HANDBOOK OF SKILLS ESSENTIAL TO BEGINNING TEACHERS

M. Serra Goethals
Bellarmine College

Rose A. Howard
Bellarmine College

UNIVERSITY
PRESS OF
AMERICA

LANHAM • NEW YORK • LONDON

British Cataloging in Publication Information Available

Library of Congress Cataloging in Publication Data
Goethals, M. Serra, 1934-
　　Handbook of skills essential to beginning
teachers.
　　Includes bibliographies and index.
　　　1. Teaching—Handbooks, manuals, etc.
　　2. Student teaching—Handbooks, manuals, etc.
　　3. Interns (Education)—Handbooks, manuals, etc.
　　I. Howard, Rose A.　　II. Title.
　　LB1025.2.G59　　1985　　　371.1'02　　　85-15664
　　ISBN 0-8191-4877-6 (alk. paper)
　　ISBN 0-8191-4878-4 (pbk. alk. paper)

All University Press of America books are produced on acid-free
paper which exceeds the minimum standards set by the National
Historical Publication and Records Commission.

Preface

In a learning-by-doing approach, the <u>Handbook of Skills Essential to Beginning Teachers</u> presents activities that apply theory to practical experience. Whether you gradually assume portions of the teacher role or abruptly take charge of instructional responsibilities, the text offers a systematic review and assessment of essential skills. Focusing on one aspect of the teaching experience allows you to recognize progress and gain confidence. This continuous application of knowledge, attitudes and theory encourages you to broadly assess your own teaching while specifically observing the individual learners in your class. Thus, this process approach provides you, as prospective teacher a framework for integrating reflection with action.

In making the initial teaching experience a most significant learning time, college and school supervisors have an extremely complex role. Knowledgeable of the teacher education program and the sequence of teaching skills essential for effective teaching, the supervisors are the link between the college and the school system for the beginning teacher. The college supervisor matches the student teaching program objectives to the teaching activities gradually assumed by the prospective teacher. Periodic classroom visits provide the supervisor an overview of the personal and professional progress of the beginning teacher.

Beginning teachers likewise benefit from an opportunity to gain an overall perspective of the new teaching experience. One vehicle used to assist student and intern teachers focus on specific objectives and competencies of the teacher education program is the seminar. Removed from the classroom environment and given the opportunity to interact with colleagues, beginning teachers examine their own progress in at least one specific aspect of teaching. Through skillful facilitation, the participants reflect on the positive aspects of growth in instructional and interaction skills. The sense of mutual sharing gained from other beginning teachers and the reviewing of appropriate behaviors and practices are both a process of self evaluation and goal setting for the future.

The authors contend that the seminar, as one approach, can provide the prospective teacher a framework for continuous review and evaluation of specific teaching behaviors and skills. Few resources exist offering teachers sequential tasks and information coordinating classroom activities, seminar topics, interaction activities and personal learning. The Handbook provides a systematic focus on particular skills which the literature deems essential for effective teaching. Reviewing and examining the practice of a single skill will more likely guarantee the beginning teacher's demonstration of this skill within the classroom setting.

The Handbook of Skills Essential to Beginning Teachers is intended for student and intern teachers, to be used individually and within group or class seminars. University and school supervisors familiar with all components of teacher preparation and those with fewer experiences will find this text suitable for class and professional use.

Contents of the text are systematically organized, beginning with obvious needs such as identifying your role and expanding toward greater sophistication and broader application of skills in succeeding chapters. Each chapter comprises two parts: 1) exercises translating theoretical teaching knowledge and skills into instructional behaviors and 2) interaction activities in which perceptions of your functioning as teacher are examined and shared with others.

The assignments contain activities for beginning teachers to complete, evidencing progress toward specific instructional skill development and preparing for discussion with supervisor, principal or seminar group. It is highly recommended that the beginning teacher keep a daily log emphasizing the suggested skill. Log excerpts address the review and practice of a skill as recorded by other beginning teachers. Further references offer the beginning teacher a broad range of resources for the topics handled in each chapter.

Observing numerous variables plaguing the beginning teacher, the authors selected and revised activities which focus on actual teaching experience. Providing a structure for the review and application of previously studied theory can further the successful integration of knowledge, attitudes and skills into classroom practice. Over the past ten years, additional modification of the materials has been made while being field tested with elementary, special education and high school beginning teachers. By enabling beginning teachers to pursue a continuous plan for becoming confident and competent professional teachers, this publication will have accomplished its mission.

Acknowledgements

We are especially appreciative and acknowledge the continuous encouragement received from distinguished colleagues.

We are grateful to former students Carol Starke, Chuck Bronson, Paula Sarver, Phil Poore, Sheila Mudd and Rob Mullen for permission to use their reflective log excerpts.

We are indebted to Leslie, Teresa and Linda for their contributed services over the years.

We dedicate this book to our first teachers, our parents, and to all teachers with whom we have shared.

Contents

1 Introduction: General Orientation

Assuming Professional Responsibility

Assuming the role of teacher creates both excitement and anxiety. Guides and directives which supply helpful information fail to quiet the fluttery feeling sensed by the beginning teacher. You may have knowledge of the teaching-learning process and have spent hours with learners in classrooms. This new role as beginning teacher, however, requires a combination of knowledge, skill, and attitudes, usually within one specific environment. While it is an opportunity to grow as person and professional teacher, the challenge can be accompanied by fear of what lies ahead.

Supported by administrative, instructional and/or university supervisory personnel, beginning teachers sequentially progress through distinctive stages of development. From being almost totally absorbed with concerns for your own success, you begin to embrace broader perspectives of the teaching-learning process. Gradually assuming greater responsibility for planning and teaching, you will develop creativity and independence in your use of techniques and materials. Having gained a sense of what should be taught, you then become concerned about how students learn and which activities and materials to use in the diagnosis and prescription for each student's achievement.

Identifying My Role

Student teachers have generally found student teaching the single most significant component of the teacher education program. This is the peak experience in which you assume an active role in the instruction of children/youth, under the direction of one or more certified and experienced teachers. It is the segment of time when knowledge, attitudes, and skills concerning teaching and learning, which mainly have been acquired on campus, are extensively applied in a school setting. Greater emphasis is placed on daily observation, participation, and actual teaching in a plan of gradual and sequential development of interpersonal and instructional skills. Quality teacher education programs establish and maintain good communication between the university and the supervising teacher, between the supervising teacher and you, and between the university supervisor and you, the student teacher. With encouragement, affirmation, honesty, and challenge among the professionals involved, your student teaching experience should prove most beneficial.

Intern teacher refers specifically to these persons having no previous experience as classroom teachers. The need for skill review or development would be the same as that required of student teachers. Except for the daily presence of the classroom teacher and the scheduled observations and conferences with the university supervisor, your role as intern teacher corresponds with that of the student teacher. Responsibility for focusing on each skill rests with you, consequently, the text provides systematic practice of these skills. Furthermore, the process approach encourages self-assessment of the knowledge, attitude and performance of those skills you will recognize as describing effective teaching.

Learning the Community and School

Knowledge of the school community and its influence on school population is essential for understanding your students. Interviewing the principal, talking with teachers, parents and students will give you a broader picture of the environmental influences and the cultural interests of the students. Obtaining an overview of the school's history and reading the school philosophy will give you new insights about your particular school. You will want to examine school goals and objectives, curriculum guides, the code of discipline and the faculty handbook. A firm grasp of the school's policies and procedures will enable you to respond to the daily school operation with greater confidence. The school and community have high expectations of their teachers, thereby placing accountability/responsibility on you to develop your talents and skill in becoming an effective teacher.

Establishing Working Relationships

Embracing the student/intern teacher role may be your initial entrance into the world of work as a professional. Students, parents, school and university personnel and colleagues in the profession have expectations specific to you as teacher. Recognizing the responsibilities and understanding other's perceptions of you as teacher influence your relationships with them.

Establishing a working relationship requires that you can effectively interact with others, whether they may be students, peer teachers or supervisors. At times you will find yourself in a power position having the role of directing other's actions and efforts. You also are expected to act as peer, planning, supporting and implementing school activities and programs. Finally, as a beginning teacher you will be called upon to demonstrate instructional and managerial skills and to show an understanding of theoretical knowledge by applying it to specific learners.

Interactions appropriate to the various kinds of relationships are not required at definite intervals nor can these be clearly delineated with specific behaviors recommended. A sorting-out and reflection process followed by a checking out of your own perceptions with peers and supervising teachers offer a needed perspective on the quality of relationships you are building. This total process extends over a period of time requiring patience with your own learning and persistent effort.

Functioning as Student/Intern Teacher

Dividing the student/intern teaching experience into four areas allows for an orderly consideration of numerous aspects of the role assumed by the prospective teacher. Each area encompasses appropriate practices initiated and continued throughout the experience and shown in Figure 1.1 for the student teacher: 1) performing in the classroom and school, 2) conferring with the supervising teacher, 3) conferencing with the college supervisor, and 4) participating in the seminar.

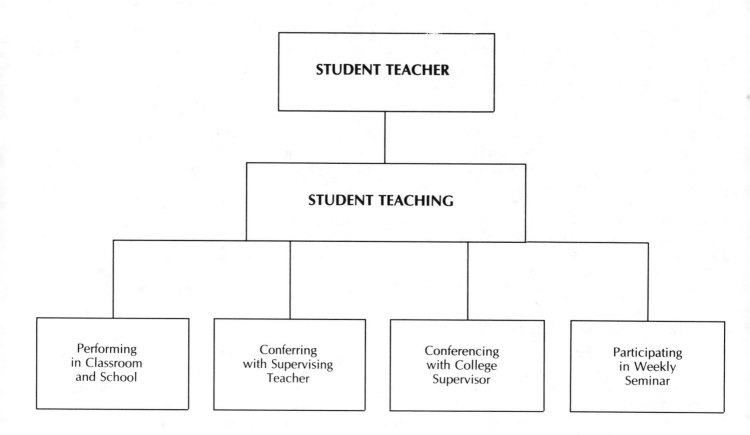

Figure 1.1
General Areas of Student Teaching

1. Performing in the Classroom and School

As student teacher, you bring a variety of intellectual and personal talents to the student teaching experience. Following a period of in-depth observation and participation, you will gradually assume responsiblity for teaching. Your lessons are planned, critiqued, revised, and sometimes retaught, with verbal and written evaluation given by your supervising teacher and college supervisor. Learning to relate to students as a teacher and to identify student strengths and weaknesses takes time. Some of you will become proficient in these skills more quickly than others. Eventually, this ability, along with that of selecting appropriate instructional materials, enables you to creatively design activities meeting the diverse interests and abilities of students. During this semester you can view the interrelatedness of the single classroom within the larger school community. Working cooperatively with other teachers, administrators and parents, you gain a sense of being a part of the total school organization.

2. Conferring with the Supervising Teacher

Your supervising teacher and you are in daily contact throughout the student teaching experience. Open communication, therefore, is vital to your successful progress. Student teachers are encouraged to meet with supervising teachers prior to beginning their experience. Developing a better understanding of the school, classroom, curriculum and student learning lessens the fear many of you may have during the early stages of student teaching. Establishing good communication creates confidence and leads to a partnership between you and your supervising teacher. Daily verbal, non-verbal and written communiques are encouraged between student and supervising teachers. Immediate feedback increases the possibility for growth in interpersonal and instructional skills.

3. Conferencing with the College Supervisor

Periodic visits made by the college supervisor give a first hand picture of the actual student teaching situation. Observations can be scheduled whereby skills and techniques are assessed and matched with the teacher education program objectives. At follow-up conferences, your supervising teacher shares written and verbal evaluative information with you. These conferences, which are essential to progress in skill development, require careful planning and structure. Whether your college supervisor uses the comments directly on certain observed techniques and behaviors or elicits this information, you need critique and suggestions as you begin to use your knowledge and judgement in making decisions about instructional strategies. As you become more comfortable, competent and confident in these conferences, self evaluative skills will surface and develop, resulting in positive goal setting.

4. Participating in the Seminar

Traditionally the college supervisor schedules a weekly seminar attended by all student teachers. The seminar is an opportunity for you to share classroom experiences thereby gaining renewed energy, ideas and focus for the following week. In addition to gaining a sense of colleagueship, participants develop the ability to analyze teaching performance, to interact openly with others about teaching and to become self directing. Weekly practice in some phase of interpersonal sharing expands the awareness of the individual's behavior and its effect upon others. In addressing questions posed during the discussions, you will accumulate insights into a variety of school settings, learner variability and teaching practices. You will learn that skills are acquired through practice and evaluation, followed by modified practice. What better time or setting for beginning this self evaluation process than in the weekly meeting? With other eager beginners, you will discover that the planned instruction and management skills may not measure up to the mental picture of how students will respond. Fear is acknowledged, discussed and worked through. Change is seen as a means for improvement, not something to avoid. Interaction skills establish among student teachers meaningful dialogue regarding aims, job satisfaction, self improvement and adaptation which enrich the organizational climate and serve as powerful vehicles for instructional improvement. This text is designed to involve you, the student teacher, in the weekly seminar activities. The activities and format are intended to help you become analytical of teaching performance, to openly interact with others about your teaching experiences and to become self directed. Without this aid you can perform teaching tasks but you may miss the keen perceptions and the broad perspectives which make student teaching an evolving, integrating and refining process.

Figure 1.2 outlines the general activities of the intern teacher totally responsible for the classroom experience: 1) contributing as faculty member, 2) performing in classroom and school, 3) demonstrating teaching behaviors for supervisory personnel, and 4) conferencing with supervisory personnel.

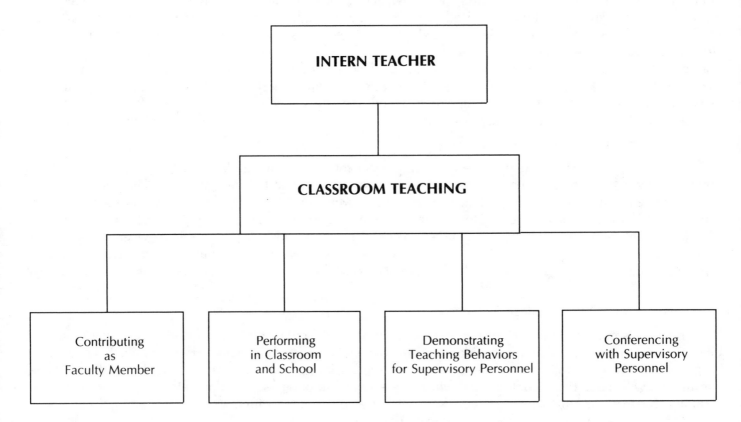

Figure 1.2
General Areas of Intern Teaching

1. Contributing as Faculty Member

As intern teacher with full responsibility as teacher you become a full time member of the school faculty. Loyalty, cooperation and honesty will be expected in your relationship with administration and other school personnel. You may be asked to work on school related committees and activities depending on your talents and expertise. Responding as a contributing member to the faculty helps build cooperation and insures the growth and development of effective schools.

2. Performing in Classroom and School

As an intern with full responsibility for teaching you will be faced with the full impact of the experience from the first day. Essential to effective teaching is good planning which takes time and energy. You will need to identify student strengths and weaknesses in order that the instructional prescriptions may be suited to student and class achievement. Understanding motivation, communicating expectations, selecting appropriate instructional materials, using reliable evaluative criteria, remediating and reteaching concepts are all part of your performance as teacher. You will begin to realize your part in the total school organization, working cooperatively with administrators, teachers and school personnel, parents and students.

3. Demonstrating Teaching Behaviors for Supervisory Personnel

Periodic visits by the administrative staff, school system supervisor and/or university personnel are scheduled to assess your instructional and interpersonal skills. The supervisory personnel may formulate or plan with you the particular teaching behaviors being assessed. You may, however, show individual initiative by presenting your own plan for developing and improving teaching techniques. In the supervisory situation there is always the need for understanding the process that aims for improvement. Establishing realistic goals and assessing the results after a specified time provides direction and allows you to mark progress in skill acquisition.

4. Conferencing with Supervisory Personnel

As follow up to the demonstration of teaching behaviors, conferences are scheduled between supervisory personnel and yourself. Written and verbal evaluative information are shared with you. Receiving assessment information and setting a plan of action to increase teaching effectiveness requires continued commitment to improvement and excellence. Acquiring open mindedness toward suggestions from supervisory personnel enables you to correctly perceive the recommendations made and to generate alternatives to existing weaknesses.

Design of the Text

The purpose of this text is to help you develop and integrate essential skills into the various components of the teaching experience. Each chapter focuses on interaction skills used in any one of the numerous exchanges a teacher has during a day or week. Some space is provided for applying this skill in a peer group situation. Emphasis is placed on your recognizing and applying the skill in routine exchanges with students and other teachers. A different instructional skill activity is also presented in each chapter. Having studied these skills in methods courses, you will need to reexamine and observe them as used by the classroom teacher. You will want to practice these skills to such an extent that teaching techniques are strengthened throughout the semester.

Developing and refining consistently desirable methods of speaking and acting within the school setting takes time. Instruction and interaction skills introduced during the first few weeks need application throughout the entire semester. Acquisition of one skill is followed by another like a snowball rolling downhill. One layer fits indiscernably onto another providing similarity in substance and noticeable growth in size and strength. Consequently appropriate change will be made in teaching behaviors when a concerted effort has been made to acquire the skills presented.

Viewing the Chapter

Each chapter is designed with the following format: 1) Interaction Activity, 2) Skill Activity, 3) Assignments for the Week, 4) Log Excerpts, and 5) Further References.

1. Interaction Activity

Activities are included on the basis of their importance to growth in communication and interpersonal skill development. Objectives are stated in behavioral terms specifying the learning outcome intended for you to demonstrate. A brief description emphasizes the importance of the objective for you personally. You will have numerous opportunities to apply this skill as a teacher.

Leaders, facilitators and others following a group process approach will find directions for establishing a setting conducive to self exploration and self disclosure. Presented in a nonthreatening tone, the activities have available commentaries directing participant attention to a single item and relating this in a personal way to their professional growth. While the text furnishes a specific focus and direction, leaders are encouraged to supplement and adapt parts and entire activities to suit group members in specific situations.

2. Skill Activity

The objectives for each chapter are stated in terms of learner outcomes, which means you are expected to plan, perform, practice and evaluate the specific skills in your classroom setting. The variety of questions offers a framework for eliciting thoughtful responses. These do not preclude questions you may have. Responding to questions stated in addition to those you raise enables you to expand your awareness and to make critical observations of the teaching-learning process. Your contribution will offer stimulation for other beginning teachers as you share your perceptions.

3. Assignment for the Week

Activities are designed so that you can systematically concentrate on specific aspects of teaching while in the classroom. Focusing on specific assignments over a given period of time will increase your awareness of how to effectively use interaction and instructional skills in varied situations.

4. Log Excerpts

Excerpts from beginning teacher logs report examples of their observations and activites. These incidents represent factual interpretation of male and female student teachers at primary, intermediate, special and secondary education levels in a variety of school settings. Reading the experiences of other beginning teachers will likely expand your perception of the skills observed and applied throughout the semester.

5. Further References

Sometimes what is included within the text will need to be supplemented with other materials. Additional texts are listed as optional resources for the topics contained in each chapter.

Processing the Content

Beginning teachers might focus on text material in a variety of ways. Used on an individual basis a single topic or series of topics and/or activities could be selected, reviewed and practiced. As student teacher you may be a member of the seminar group. Because you are participants in different segments of the school system i.e., elementary, middle, high school, special education, and teaching in various geographic locations, your comments, views and/or discussion reflect and strengthen relationships modeling the concept of mainstreaming in the schools. Your responses are notable and valuable to others in developing different perspectives. Distancing yourself from your placement, looking at the situation objectively and listening to other student teachers relate feelings, experiences and learnings will add new dimensions to your conceptualization of the teaching process. Integrating skills essential to teaching is a relationed process as exhibited in Figure 1.3.

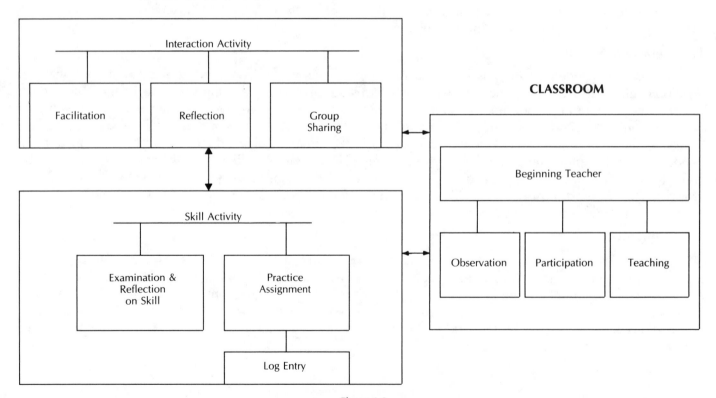

Figure 1.3

Integration of Skills into the Teaching Process

Theory and skills which you previously studied are now examined and applied to classroom activities planned for specific learners. Practice modification and repeated practice determine the level of integration attained by the beginning teacher.

In order to become an effective teacher, a high level of interpersonal functioning is essential. As a beginning teacher, you will be conversing with students, teachers and parents, as well as with administrative and supervisory staff, in face-to-face settings, in committees and in large organizational groups. These interactions will require skills in listening, interpreting, eliciting and conveying information.

The interaction activities have been designed to help you establish, maintain and practice, within a short period of time, effective interpersonal skills which contribute a positive mental health. Emphasis is placed on accomplishments, acquired skills and abilities. Reflection time is essential, enabling you to carefully order your thoughts and comments before sharing with others.

During your methods and curriculum courses, you have examined and practiced specific skills within a designated time and setting. Your initial teaching time will offer extended practice in which to integrate these skills on a day to day basis. Designating specific skills, evaluating your progress, reinforcing your efforts, sharing your successes and limitations in achieving these skills are processes leading to effective teaching.

2 Getting Organized

INTERACTION ACTIVITY: Initiating Conversation

Objective

To introduce oneself and to apply listening techniques.

Coming together for the first time as individuals about to begin teaching is an opportunity to examine a few common experiences. Realizing that you are not alone in new surroundings can buoy you up for the week ahead and help you meet the responsibilities outlined in this chapter. Good communication with others is among the responsibilities considered essential to teaching.

Effective communication skills can be acquired and strengthened given sufficient time and effort. Reserving space in the routine for weekly reflection and practice, you create an awareness of your own interactions. You, then, are better able to apply and modify verbal and nonverbal communication skills in your interactions with others in the school.

Demonstrate your willingness to interact with those around you. Introduce yourself to another beginning teacher whom you do not know or with whom you infrequently converse. Volunteer information about yourself such as where you will be living and teaching; tell about your earlier practicum experiences. Besides initiating conversation also practice good listening techniques. While another is talking, position yourself so as to face the person paying attention to the total message. Hear the expression and pitch of the other person's voice, be aware of body movements, breathing and amount of eye contact. Consider your use of the same characteristics when speaking to one person and to a group.

Directions and Procedures

Leader of the group sets the tone by:

1. Directing the group to arrange chairs in a circle so that all (20 or fewer persons) can be accommodated as a single unit, each participant visible to others.
2. Emphasizing the significance of communication skills to teaching.
3. Explaining that quality participation within the group depends on the extent individuals enter into the reflection and sharing exercises. It is possible over a period of time for the group to create a climate of genuine listening and honest responding to each other.

Leader: Introducing another person to a group is oftentimes easier than introducing oneself. Spending a few minutes interviewing one member of a group and then giving the entire group some factual information about this person quickly enlarges the number of persons you are likely to remember. Through introductions and interview information, you come to know about each person in your group.

For this activity select another teacher whom you know less well or not at all. Then, take turns asking the other about him/herself i.e. name, residence, work experiences, hobbies, school where s/he will be teaching.

(Encourage members to move around, seek out a partner. Allow approximately 4 minutes for the interchange, then reassemble the group into the circular formation.)

Leader: In introducing your partner recall the person's name and some key facts you learned. Using someone's name in conversation better enables you to recall that name at a later time.

(Introduction of group members. After all have been introduced, the Leader may offer the opportunity for individuals to name all members. Discussion questions presented the total group require that participants make application of the interaction activity to the teacher's role.)

Leader: Before making comparison with the use of names in this group and the classroom; think about how you listened while the other person talked. To what extent were you able to gain information about the other in addition to hearing words?

Discussion Questions

Leader: A. As a prospective teacher, why are names important?

B. How well do you remember names?

C. What mental schemes have you developed to help you learn the names of students?

SKILL ACTIVITY: **Organization**

Objectives

To organize, plan and follow directions for entering the teaching role.
To log daily observation and school experiences.

You are about to step into the peak experience of your teacher education program. To facilitate organization and planning for this important time, the following are offered for your consideration and action:

1. Call the principal and supervising teacher of your school prior to appearing at the school.
   a. Introduce yourself as beginning or student teacher.
   b. Let the principal know you would like to be present for any meetings held prior to the first day of class. Ask that you be informed of dates and times. These meetings can be essential to your becoming partner teacher or member of the faculty in the school setting.
2. Keep a schedule of all important dates to remember. Be on time and appear as professional for any meetings.
3. Work as partner with your supervising or team teacher in such activities as:
   a. arranging the classroom
   b. scheduling classes
   c. preparing materials
   d. designing bulletin boards.
(The more you put into your assignment, the more you will receive!)
4. Examine the Student Teacher Handbook from your university. You may have questions regarding the required competencies, the legal status of your role of personnel involved in the student/intern teacher experience.
5. Record the time spent in observation, participation and actual teaching experience. The log of hours form for this activity can be found on page 14. You may want to make extra copies depending on the length of your experience.
6. Enter the observations, reflections, activities and suggestions made each day on the assignment sheets (or in a separate log). Reporting from other beginning teacher observations are included in each chapter examples for your own writing.

* * * * *

Assignment (Observing the Teaching Learning Process)

Developing skills for conceptualizing what teachers are doing, comes with practice. Your pre-service observations have equipped you with specific skill in analyzing and labeling classroom behavior. Daily practice in identifying and labeling specific teaching skills will help you to become aware of your own classroom behavior and improve your teaching skill. This week you will direct your observations and written comments to specific aspects of the teaching learning environment.

Log your observations and responses to the topics listed below. The specific topics serve as guides. Add any other descriptive information you consider valuable to the observation.

Outstanding physical features of the school building including all areas used by learners:

_____

_____

_____

_____

_____

_____

_____

_____

_____

_____

Physical features of the classroom used including:

chalkboard space_____

_____

_____

bulletin boards_____

_____

_____

desk arrangement_____

_____

_____

lighting_____

_____

_____

displays _____

_____

_____

Arrangements made for special learners:

equipment _____

_____

_____

special meetings _____

_____

_____

classroom arrangement _____

_____

_____

schedule arrangement _____

_____

_____

Describe the supervising or team teacher approach and manner with students:

personal
characteristics _____

_____

_____

appearance _____

_____

_____

communication skill _____

_____

_____

voice _____

_____

_____

eye contact _____

_____

_____

facial expression _____

_____

Describe the student overall response to the supervising or team teachers:

_____

_____

_____

_____

_____

_____

_____

_____

_____

_____

_____

_____

_____

_____

_____

_____

_____

_____

_____

_____

_____

_____

_____

_____

_____

_____

_____

Log of Hours

Month _____   Name _____

Monday	Tuesday	Wednesday	Thursday	Friday

observed: _____
participated: _____
taught: _____
    other
    activities
	o _____
	p _____
	t _____
		o _____
		p _____
		t _____
			o _____
			p _____
			t _____
				o _____
				p _____
				t _____

observed: _____
participated: _____
taught: _____
    other
    activities
	o _____
	p _____
	t _____
		o _____
		p _____
		t _____
			o _____
			p _____
			t _____
				o _____
				p _____
				t _____

observed: _____
participated: _____
taught: _____
    other
    activities
	o _____
	p _____
	t _____
		o _____
		p _____
		t _____
			o _____
			p _____
			t _____
				o _____
				p _____
				t _____

observed: _____
participated: _____
taught: _____
    other
    activities
	o _____
	p _____
	t _____
		o _____
		p _____
		t _____
			o _____
			p _____
			t _____
				o _____
				p _____
				t _____

observed: _____
participated: _____
taught: _____
    other
    activities
	o _____
	p _____
	t _____
		o _____
		p _____
		t _____
			o _____
			p _____
			t _____
				o _____
				p _____
				t _____

observed: _____
participated: _____
taught: _____
    other
    activities
	o _____
	p _____
	t _____
		o _____
		p _____
		t _____
			o _____
			p _____
			t _____
				o _____
				p _____
				t _____

Log of Hours

Month _____   Name _____

Monday	Tuesday	Wednesday	Thursday	Friday

observed: _____
participated: _____
taught: _____
      other
      activities
	o _____
	p _____
	t _____
		o _____
		p _____
		t _____
			o _____
			p _____
			t _____
				o _____
				p _____
				t _____

observed: _____
participated: _____
taught: _____
      other
      activities
	o _____
	p _____
	t _____
		o _____
		p _____
		t _____
			o _____
			p _____
			t _____
				o _____
				p _____
				t _____

observed: _____
participated: _____
taught: _____
      other
      activities
	o _____
	p _____
	t _____
		o _____
		p _____
		t _____
			o _____
			p _____
			t _____
				o _____
				p _____
				t _____

observed: _____
participated: _____
taught: _____
      other
      activities
	o _____
	p _____
	t _____
		o _____
		p _____
		t _____
			o _____
			p _____
			t _____
				o _____
				p _____
				t _____

observed: _____
participated: _____
taught: _____
      other
      activities
	o _____
	p _____
	t _____
		o _____
		p _____
		t _____
			o _____
			p _____
			t _____
				o _____
				p _____
				t _____

observed: _____
participated: _____
taught: _____
      other
      activities
	o _____
	p _____
	t _____
		o _____
		p _____
		t _____
			o _____
			p _____
			t _____
				o _____
				p _____
				t _____

Log Excerpts (Observing the Teaching Learning Environment)

I like the room--it is very oriented toward the children. It is neat yet reflects Mrs. A.'s enthusiasm and interest in children. I cut out letters and decorated bulletin boards. The most interesting part of the whole day was getting to know Mrs. A. She has so many great ideas and her attitude is one the light side. She takes her job seriously as it should be taken yet is always ready to laugh to herself about the students. I think that kind of frame of mind must relax her and the children especially.

*****

Miss B. had the children talk about the things all over the room: bulletin boards, fire alarm, reading chairs, alphabet. Explains what each thing is for, even the ideas behind the bulletin board, such as racquets and balls with heading "Swing into Second Grade." Consequently, the children are already involved in the structure items. By asking the children questions, instead of talking in a monologue or lecturing, the children discuss classroom behavior, manners, learning what is expect of them in the classroom.

*****

Half hour periods today. Introduced as teacher (not student teacher), which I appreciated. Students placed in alphabetical order in the hopes of learning names easier. Learning names will be a formidable task! Mr. D. explained the textbooks being used in his class (e.g. folder, spiral notebook). Finally, explained the grading system, tests, etc. As an activity, he passed out a Following Directions assignment to the freshmen and a background information sheet to the juniors--also gave homework. I felt fairly useful today. I was even able to open some troublesome lockers. Mr. D. was well prepared. All of the students' materials were lying on their alphabetized desks when they walked in. (I helped distribute this material.)

*****

While Mr. C. called roll, I made out seating chart, leaving some open desks up front for students with sight/hearing problems if they choose to move. Time flew by--Mr. C. was correctly prepared. He moves with the assurance of experience.

*****

Mrs. G. has a number of techniques to reinforce and control the class. The first is the Friendship Club. You must follow a list of rules to belong to this club plus new officers are elected every month or so and you must have been a good member. Also, Mrs. G. gives out play money as rewards and every few months has a sale. This really excited the children. I think it is an excellent idea. The children behave, do extra work, remember to bring homework the next day, etc. with a monetary incentive. Plus, Mrs. G. wil later get into taxes, rent for their condominiums (desks) and other real life facts.

Further References

Flanders, Ned A. Analyzing Teacher Behavior. Reading, Massachusettes: Addison-Wesley, 1970.

Gazda, George, Frank R. Asbury, Fred J. Balzer, et al. Human Relations Development: A Manual for Educators, 2nd ed. Boston: Allyn and Bacon, 1977.

Good, Thomas L. and Jere E. Brophy. Looking in Classrooms, 3rd ed. New York: Harper & Row, 1984.

Gordon, Thomas. Teacher Effectiveness Training. New York: David McKay Company, 1974.

Roe, Betty D., Ross, Elinor P., Burns, Paul C. Student Teaching and Field Experiences Handbook. Columbus, Ohio: Charles E. Merrill Publishing Company, 1984.

Soar, Robert S. and Ruth M. Soar, "Observing the Classroom." In Introduction to Education, pp. 163-198. Edited by Donald E. Orlosky. Columbus, Ohio: Charles E. Merrill Publishing Company, 1982

Stallings, Jane A. Learning to Look. Belmont, California: Wadsworth, 1977.

3 Observing the Teaching Learning Process

INTERACTION ACTIVITY: **Write Perception**

Objective
To express in writing individual perceptions of the teaching role.

As a beginning teacher you are probably feeling an array of different emotions. Significant to your benefitting from the time spent learning to teach, is the ability to distance yourself from the specifics of the classroom in order to consider the following:

individual strengths
process of learning to teach,
professional role to which you aspire.

This interaction activity is intended to help you list and reflect upon specific requirements of teachers. Recall from research the characteristics of effective teachers. Focus, also, on abilities you possess and which you demonstrated when working with children and youth in schools and in other settings.

Directions and Procedures

Leader sets the tone by:

1. Directing the group into a suitable physical arrangement.
2. Emphasizing that participation and initiation within the group is similar to new teachers' behaviors in the classroom and school.
3. Explain that getting to know oneself is an essential component of professional as well as personal growth.
4. Furnishing group members with blank sheets of paper (page from text might be removed) for answering the three questions. If meetings are held weekly or at regular intervals, the leader may distribute an envelope for keeping responses private. The envelope will be returned during a session some weeks later.

Leader: Take some time to write your responses to each of the three questions given below. Write freely. The written messages are for you; no one else needs to know your thoughts. You will have 5 minutes or enough time for writing a response to each question.

1. What aspect of the teaching role do you see as most important? _____

_____

_____

_____

_____

_____

_____

_____

2. What is the most difficult aspect of the teaching role as you perceive it at this time? _____

_____

_____

_____

_____

_____

_____

3. What do you as beginning teacher bring to the school and classroom? _____

_____

_____

_____

_____

_____

_____

[Distribute envelopes and direct participants to enclose response sheets, seal and write their names on the envelopes for later identification. Before collecting the envelopes assure the participants that they will be returned unopened.]

Leader: For this interaction activity again choose another person whom you know least well, if possible, select someone with a teaching assignment in a subject area/grade level different from yours. First, think about the questions you just answered and the responses you wrote. Before beginning to talk in your dyads recall that good listening is more than being silent. Give your total attention to the speaker. While speaking focus on the message you want to send and the receiver—keep eye contact. Here are some points to share.

1. Which response came more easily?
2. Which questions seemed difficult for you?
3. If there were differences in the level of difficulty, why is one question harder for you to answer than another?

[Allow 4-6 minutes, then, call the total group together and focus attention on the process. Pause in order to encourage individual response to each question.]

Discussion Questions

A. Consider what occurred when you and your partner were sharing. While listening did you recognize similarities between what you and your partner found easy? Difficult?
B. How did you feel when you heard the other person express thoughts and feelings which were the same as yours?

Leader: Realizing that others have the same thoughts and feelings often encourages and strengthens trust in your own perceptions. As beginning teachers you will face many situations in which you will need to trust your perceptions and to act. In the following days be aware of how your perceptions impact your actions.

A final reflection point on this activity is to briefly assess listening skills. In order to correctly perceive classroom events the ability to listen is of major importance. Think about the kind of listener you were to your partner; how well did you listen? How difficult was it to keep your attention on what the other person was saying? Did you look directly at the person while s/he was talking? Did you give him/her equal time or did you say, ''Yes, that reminds me of the time I . . .'' and began telling something from your own experience? Did your comments indicate to your partner that you heard what was said. A second skill to practice during the next week is active listening.

18

SKILL ACTIVITY: **Observation**

Objectives
To observe specific teacher behaviors, the classroom environment and instructional organization.
To assist in providing an attractive and orderly learning environment.

During this past week you have begun some specific observation within your student teaching placement. Using your log entry and recalling events from the past week, share your response to the following questions:

1. What are the outstanding physical features of the school, the classroom, the other areas used by students?
2. How does the teacher's appearance, personality, voice and communication skills affect the learning climate in the classroom?
3. What expectations of student behavior are evident? How are these communicated to students?
4. How did students know the first learning tasks or procedure for the day?
5. How were you introduced to the class? In what ways did you contribute to the progress of the students in their orientation to the class environment?

Additional questions may surface. It will be evident from the participation in discussion how observant you have become.

Assignment (Participating in the Planning Process)

The task of planning for classroom instruction requires knowledge of the planning process and skill in decision making. You need a framework which will aid you in this planning process. Competent teachers use the following steps in planning for teaching:

1. diagnosis and assessment of student needs,
2. development of objectives including both long and short term goals,
3. organization of content, materials and students,
4. facilitation of learners, content and environment,
5. evaluation to determine learner outcomes,
6. remediation and/or subsequent instruction.

You may want to review grouping patterns, methods for diagnosing learner strengths and weaknesses and the procedure for referring special learners within the school. Essential to preparation is background knowledge of subject taught. Reading texts and other supplementary materials will give depth to the topics presented.

This week's assignment focuses on preliminary identification of learner ability and examination of instructional resources.

1. Examine the grouping of students and the diagnostic procedures for determining the needs and problems of learners in your class(es). List the kinds of information collected on individual differences including:

    student interests _____

    _____

    _____

    academic ability _____

    _____

    _____

reading levels _____

_____

_____

verbal and written language skills _____

_____

_____

2. Study the texts and other materials used for your classes. List title, publisher, and copyright date for one text used regularly.

_____

_____

_____

using the text named above, comment on the following level of reading difficulty (approximate) _____

_____

_____

_____

illustrative materials (maps, pictures, diagrams) _____

_____

_____

attractiveness and appeal _____

_____

_____

3. Volunteer to assume routine tasks: taking role, grading papers, designing a seating chart, tutoring, etc. Describe your participation.

_____

_____

_____

_____

_____

_____

_____

_____

_____

Log Excerpts (Participating in the Planning Process)

I filled in the names of the children and the absences in Mrs. A.'s roll book. I also checked the sentences the children wrote using their spelling words. It was interesting to note a child's handwriting and creativity in making up the sentences.

*****

While Ms. C. taught her lessons, I went downstairs and reviewed some special education curriculum guides concerned with math, language arts, and boardwork ideas. I brought two of them home with me to become even more familiar with them.

*****

I looked through the SER Guide (Special Expectations in Reading). Is very idealistic. Would be nice if truly implemented.

*****

I used the seating chart today to call out names of students wishing to answer one of Mr. C's given questions—this worked out really well, as I became familiar with students by the time the period ended. Will definitely know more names tomorrow. Have become amazed at how little of the day is wasted—there is almost constant occupation in one form or another. Juniors can be intimidating if one allows them to be. Yet, they show marvelous cooperation in most cases. One must remember that they're good kids and are really not interested in itimidation. Respect will be gained from excellently run classes.

*****

So far the freshman provide a plethora of interesting behavior. They seem genuinely frightened right now and, as a result, provide little discipline problem. Yet, freshman teachers must be really observant, I feel, because freshman are very reluctant to say anything if something is troubling them or if they aren't following things. They seem to need a little more help and understanding at this point than do the older students. The juniors, on the other hand, have my respect for different reasons. They have, I feel, the most difficult course schedule, and are in the difficult position of being old-timers in the school without any of the benefits of seniority. I think it takes really top notch classes to stimulate juniors, yet such excellent classes will yield excellent results from this highly primed group of students. (College is becoming an important reality for many of them and they are growing more mature as a result.) Mr. D. has spent a lot of time, I feel, reminding them that he is in charge. There can already be no doubt of his expectations—high expectations will, hopefully, produce excellent behavior. One sees, in the junior classes, the effects of afterschool jobs and later hours. The faces look a little more haggard and there is a lot more yawning (also attributed to 5th and 6th periods). They are a sharp bunch of students who probably work harder than any other grade level in the school. Good classes should produce excellent results with juniors -- poor classes could be disasterous; they will not tolerate them, which is actually a very good thing.

*****

I attended the SBARC meeting with Ms. C. The first grade teacher, Ms. C., the counselor, the speech teacher, and the girl's mother were present for the meeting. Her I.Q. score was in the EMH range, but her performance in class and adaptive behavior is "normal." Therefore, they agreed to keep her in the regular class with speech therapy. Her progress will be reviewed again in January.

*****

Miss B. is giving them a pre-test to find out where they are in Math. Before she gave it to them, she explained what a pre-test is, attempting to assure them that if they don't know how to do something or can't remember how, this is OK. She just wants to know what they know or where they are. Something cute she did: compared pre-test to a preview before a movie—helpful to the children's comprehension of the word. Explaining the directions to each question carefully and separately. Very helpful to the students.

*****

I now do the milk money in the morning. How can something simple get complicated? I was a nickel short. Tomorrow I will make sure the kids stay in their seats and get the correct change.

Further References

Good, Thomas L. and Jere E. Brophy. Looking in Classroom, 3rd ed. New York: Harper and Row, 1984.

Hamachek, Don E. Encounters With the Self, 2nd ed. Chicago: Holt, Rinehart and Winston, 1978.

Hoover, Kenneth H. Professional Teacher's Handbook: A Guide for Improving Instruction in Today's Middle and Secondary Schools, 3rd ed. Boston: Allyn and Bacon, 1982.

Jacobsen, David, Paul Eggen, Donald Kauchak, et al. Methods for Teaching, 2nd ed. Columbus: Charles E. Merrill Publishing Company, 1985.

Jarolimek, John and Clifford D. Foster. Teaching and Learning in the Elementary School, 2nd ed. New York: Macmillan Publishing Company, 1981.

Jersild, Arthur T. When Teachers Face Themselves. Columbia University, Teachers College, 1955.

Morine-Dershimer and Jeanne Pfeifer. "Instructional Planning." In James M. Cooper, general edition. Classroom Teaching Skills, Lexington, Massachusetts: D.C. Heath and Company, 1982.

Posner, George. Field Experience: A Guide to Reflective Teaching. New York: Longman, 1984.

Ryan, Kevin and James M. Cooper. Those Who Can, Teach, 4th ed. Boston: Houghton, Mifflin and Company, 1984.

4 Participating in the Planning Process

INTERACTION ACTIVITY: Assessing Your Teaching Role

Objective

To cite one incident supporting the assessment of your role in the classroom.

Self evaluation or assessment begins early and is an ongoing process. To look back at a situation and to see yourself in an objective manner is an especially important ability for pre and inservice teachers. Only after objectively perceiving your own behavior can you begin to assess the appropriateness of this behavior. Self assessment is important for you as a beginning teacher and in your continuing role as a professional.

This interaction activity presents self assessment by having you select one specific incident, recall the circumstances involved and relate that incident to some facet of the teacher role. Being willing to consider factual information, positive as well as negative, enables you to generate alternatives and enhances the assessment process.

Directions and Procedures

Leader sets the tone by:

1. Directing the group into a suitable physical arrangement.
2. Calling attention to the intended outcome of the reflection process and encouraging participants to use the process as a review of behavior and skills to practice.

Leader: For this activity picture yourself in the classroom one day during a specific time within the last few days. Review your role. With your minds eye view yourself as though seeing yourself through a camera lens. In what part of the room were you? Look at the students and mentally recall the connection between their activity and you. Even though you may not have been directing the activity, what was going on in your head? To what extent were you engaged or not engaged in the activity? Spend a few minutes now recalling the last few days and identify a single incident. Then, assess your role as demonstrated by certain teacher behaviors you practiced or that you target for future practice.

[Allow 2-4 minutes for individual reflection before directing the group into sharing their perceptions with one other person.]

Leader: Look about the group and select another member whom you know little or not at all. Move into a dyad and each take a turn describing the incident you recalled from a few days ago. When speaking keep mindful of the message you want to convey. While the other speaks, listen attentively to all that is being said. With your gestures and comments let others know they are being heard.

[After 4-6 minutes call the total group together. If the members seem comfortable, ask for large group sharing of discussion questions.]

Discussion Questions

Leader: A. What descriptions or characteristics of the teaching role were mentioned by either of you?
B. In what way did your incident relate to your partner's?
Complement each other?
C. You reflected, identified one incident from your past performance and listened to others describe how they see themselves as beginning teachers. What carry over might this have for you in the coming days?

SKILL ACTIVITY: **Planning**

Objectives

To identify individual differences among learners.
To read and examine texts and supplementary materials used for instruction.

Focusing on specific incidents in the teaching learning process can be difficult. Gathering information concerning student interests, achievement levels and language ability helps you learn that variations and adjustments are necessary in planning for individual differences among children and youth. Use the following questions as focus:

1. In what way did you assist or direct students during opening exercises?
2. How is the school day organized to schedule special students from your classes?
3. How is "on task" time handled by the teacher when students are leaving during class time?
4. Do you know the names of all students in your class(es)? What means of recall have you used to remember names?
5. Take at least two classes and describe the quality of performance expected from the students. What sources did you use to help you accumulate information concerning learner differences?
6. What access do teachers in your school have to resources kept in the library materials center? Is there any special system for request or checkout?
7. Having read and examined the textbooks for your classes, list additional materials you will need for effectively communicating content for each class.

*****

Assignment (Planning for Instruction)

Essential to good planning for instruction is the demonstrated ability to write instructional objectives. If you are going to become an effective teacher you must know what you want your students to accomplish. In other words when you as teacher have clearly defined goals and objectives students will know what is expected of them. Gradually, with reinforcement, students will become more self evaluative and set high expectations themselves.

You may formulate good instructional objectives at this time without any additional practice. Some textbooks include objectives appropriate to a particular grade level and these may be helpful to you in formulating objectives for your students.

For those of you who want a review of the components for writing instructional objectives keep in mind the following points:
1. Emphasize the instructional objective is learner oriented:
   ex.   The <u>student</u> will be able to select the main idea from a paragraph provided by the teacher.
2. Determine what the learner will accomplish, i.e., learner outcome. (Is it stated clearly and in observable terms?)
   ex.   Given a list of organisms found in a particular tropical ecosystem (old lake, inland lake, beach, coral reef) <u>place the organisms in the order in which they would occur over time, from the pioneer community to the climax community.</u>
3. Set the acceptable criteria for assessing the level of performance.
   ex.   Given 5 examples students will be able to multiple two digit numbers by one-digit numbers with <u>80% percent accuracy.</u>

Resources listed at the end of this chapter contain detailed information and provide background instruction for those needing additional help. With practice in writing clear and observable instructional objectives, beginning teachers, observing other teachers, can recognize what objectives have been determined for a specific lesson taught. The assignment below gives practice in observing and writing instructional objectives for the learner within your classes.

1. List instructional objectives for at least one class each day. For the objectives listed, which activities were planned to provide the teacher written or verbal evidence of the learning outcome? Describe the techniques you observe or use this week to reach the desired learning outcome, i.e. lecture, discussion, role playing, drill, etc.

   a. Subject _____ Class Size _____

   Objective _____

   _____

   Evidence of Learning Outcome _____

   Teaching Techniques _____

   _____

   b. Subject _____ Class Size _____

   Objective _____

   _____

   Evidence of Learning Outcome _____

   Teaching Techniques _____

   _____

   c. Subject _____ Class Size _____

   Objective _____

   _____

   Evidence of Learning Outcome _____

   Teaching Techniques _____

   _____

Beginning teachers vary in ability to initiate and participate in instructional tasks within the classroom. Giving directions can be a first step in the process of building your confidence. Determine whether you are able to detect the difference between students having difficulty following directions and those learners with limited listening skill.

2. Volunteer to give directions for one class or activity.
   a. Considerations for stating explicit directions:

   _____

   _____

   _____

   _____

   _____

   _____

   _____

   _____

b. Difficulties you perceived in giving clear directions:

_____

_____

_____

_____

_____

_____

c. Difficulties you observed students exhibiting in following directions:

_____

_____

_____

_____

_____

_____

_____

_____

_____

_____

_____

_____

_____

_____

_____

_____

_____

_____

_____

_____

Log Excerpts (Planning for Instruction)

In English, the behavioral objective may be "given a sentence on the board, the students will verablly tell the noun, verb, pronoun, adverb and objective." The children know what the objective is—they know what is expected of them. Even though this is the same material they have been covering since last week, they are excited—full participation.

Mrs. A. gave an opening sentence of a paragraph. "My room is the (messiest/neatest). . ." Objective: The student will creatively write a paragraph, giving a starting sentence. It is clear to the kids, to her, and to the observer.

*****

I think the spelling lesson went well! Although it was only a one sentence thing, my motivation made the activity fun for the children. They really did enjoy it—and understood it! I did make a mistake when I began, however, by not making sure everybody had their books out and were ready before I started to talk and then had to stop so Missy and Matthew could find the place.

*****

Math—worked on regrouping with straws. The kids are having trouble doing large subtraction problems. This was a semi-concrete way to explain regrouping. It was a visual aid, too, for those who are visually oriented.

*****

My gosh! In as much detail as Mrs. B. explained the directions this morning, I didn't think there would be any problems. Two of the children have begun to write on the laminated pages. While Ms. B. is giving the directions for the math page, she is constantly in tune with what is going on with each of the students—placing her hand on Missy's head to get her attention, turning Patrick around in his seat, providing Claire with a way to obtain a pencil, etc. Good!

*****

One of the problems with teaching English, I'm convinced is that often one's directions cannot be totally specific—there are simply too darn many exceptions! I'm beginning to realize the importance of being as specific/consistent with my directions as I can be—lay down the law and stick to it, so to speak. Making exceptions, I've found, breeds disrespect for responsibility in students, and that simply will not do when excellence is being expected. Live and learn.

*****

Well, I goofed again! Mr. C. gave directions which I didn't hear and I turned around and gave different directions.

Further References

Bloom, Benjamin S., editor. Taxonomy of Education Objectives: Cognitive Domain. New York: McKay, 1956.

Burns, Richard W. New Approaches to Behavioral Objectives. Dubuque, Iowa: William C. Brown, 1972.

Clark, Leonard H. and Irving S. Starr. Secondary and Middle School Teaching Methods, 4th ed. New York: Macmillan Publishing Company, 1981.

Gronlund, Norman E. Stating Behavioral Objectives for Classroom Instruction. New York: Macmillan, 1970.

Henson, Kenneth T. Secondary Teaching Methods. Lexington: D. C. Heath and Company, 1981.

Jacobsen, David, Paul Eggen, Donald Kauchak, et. al. Methods for Teaching a Skills Approach, 2nd ed. Columbus, Ohio: Charles E. Merrill, 1985.

Kibler, Robert J. Barker, Larry L. and Miles, David T. Behavioral Objectives and Instruction: Boston: Allyn and Bacon, 1970.

Krathwohl, David R., Bloom, Benjamin S. and Masia, Bertram B. Taxonomy of Education Objectives: Affective Domain. New York: McKay, 1964.

Mager, Robert F. Preparing Instructional Objectives, second edition. Palo Alto, California: Fearson, 1976.

Tenebrink, Terry D. Evaluation: A Practical Guide for Teachers. New York: McGraw-Hill Book Company, 1974.

5 Planning for Instruction

INTERACTION ACTIVITY: Overwhelming Pursuit

Objective

To correctly identify incidents of feeling overwhelmed.

While teaching, it is possible to learn much about yourself. The ability to recognize the feelings within yourself, to correctly identify or label emotions, is an important learning. Labeling does not mean venting or responding with aggressive emotions. In a professional setting such behavior is inappropriate. Labeling emotions is only a first step; next you choose actions and make decisions based on rational thinking rather than feelings.

At one time or another beginning teachers, like veteran teachers, feel overwhelmed. Occurring some weeks after initial fears have subsided, the sense of bewilderment gradually emerges. This interaction actitivity invites you to reflect on the feeling of bewilderment, of being overwhelmed, and, to label these and other feelings you have.

Directions and Procedures

[After directing participant attention to the group arrangement, the Leader introduces the interaction activity.]

Leader: After some weeks as a beginning teacher you better understand the demands of planning, teaching and following student progress. Some stardust has settled and teacher responsibilities seem to extend endlessly. How much walking, standing and talking you do! Anticipating, remembering, reminding and doing fill each school day. What seemed logical to your head, how a thing should be done, is not the way you behave. So much energy and effort is demanded.
Can you think of a time you felt bombarded with such thoughts?
How did you feel?
Did you recognize it as feeling overwhelmed? bewildered?

Take a few minutes to recall at least one incident of feeling overwhelmed, bewildered. Focus your thoughts on what you were feeling.

[Allow 2-4 minutes for quiet reflection time.]

Leader: In earlier group sharing you found that others' experiences were similar to your own. Now that you have pondered and labeled feelings as a beginner, turn or move near another person and relate a situation beginning the phrase with, "I felt overwhelmed. . ." While describing the incident, use words which convey feelings (i.e. distressed, doubtful, swamped, helpless, uneasy, fidgety, anxious). Be an attentive listener to your partner.

[Allow 5-6 minutes and then call together the total group.]

Discussion Questions

Leader: Large group sharing provides further comments on the points reflected upon and exchanged during the interaction activity. As part of the group you contribute and benefit from quality exchange among the members. Just as no member should feel total responsibility for keeping the discussion going, so should no one leave the talking to others in the group. Here are some questions for you as a group to consider. Exchange insights which you may have.

Leader: A. In what ways were your experiences similar to that of your partner?
B. When you learned that others have similar happenings, in what way did it affect your talking about your own experiences?
C. How would you describe your own listening ability at this time?
D. What are some feelings you have when others listen to you?

SKILL ACTIVITY: **Planning Instruction**

Objectives
To identify learner objectives, teaching procedures, skills practiced, materials used and evaluative feedback.
To give clear directions and explanations related to lesson content.

Planning effective lessons for a specific group of learners requires demonstrated ability to write instructional objectives. Through your observation and recording of instructional objectives you are developing insight concerning lesson planning and learner achievement. Formulating plans for determining which teaching procedures and materials are to be used for the content being presented and deciding the means of evaluating the lesson take practice. The following activity will assist you in sharing your assignment:

1. Select one objective you observed or recorded. Describe the procedure used to obtain the desired learner outcome and state whether the observable performance was written or verbal.
2. List the varied teaching techniques used for the different content areas and for exceptional students.
3. Describe one skill presented during a lesson. Did the learners receive individual or group reinforcement? What instructional materials were used in the presentation?
4. Give an example of directions you stated for learners. What factors helped students in following your directions?
5. When you reworded explanations of content, what was the outcome for the learner?

*****

Assignment (Presenting the Lesson)

Presentation of content requires communication skills of the beginning teacher. Most learning theorists and practitioners use their own variation of some 25 identified lesson presentation skills. Introduction to the lesson or set induction, reinforcement techniques used to achieve learning and closure methods to emphasize major points in a lesson are the most frequently researched skills you will practice as you begin to direct the teaching learning process. Focusing and keeping the learners attention to the lesson content takes creativity and planning. Varying the presentation and maintaining a high level of learner participation requires knowledge of subject matter and familiarity with various interaction techniques. Helping the learner organize the content presented to them and emphasizing the key points to be learned and retained for future use takes careful planning and timing. The following assignment affords you opportunity to observe and practice the introductory, reinforcing and concluding activities of lessons taught.

Each day choose a class to observe and record the following:

Date _____ Class _____ Teacher _____

Introduction (Set Induction)

_____

_____

_____

Reinforcement techniques

_____

_____

_____

Closure methods

_____

_____

_____

_____

Date _____ Class _____ Teacher _____

Introduction (Set Induction)

_____

_____

_____

Reinforcement techniques

_____

_____

_____

_____

Closure methods

_____

_____

_____

_____

Date _____ Class _____ Teacher _____

Introduction (Set Induction)

_____

_____

_____

Reinforcement techniques

_____

_____

_____

_____

Closure methods

_____

_____

_____

_____

Date_____ Class_____ Teacher_____

Introduction (Set Induction)

_____

_____

_____

Reinforcement techniques

_____

_____

_____

_____

Closure methods

_____

_____

_____

_____

Log Excerpts (Presenting the Lesson)

The Floats reading group is starting a new story. Introducing new words in phrases. Before reading the story, Ms. B. asks the students to close their eyes and imagine that they are lying down in their backyards. "Start out on your backs and then turn over on your stomachs. What do you see, what can you touch, what do you hear?" Then they talk about it. Very creative!

*****

Tried to observe set induction in Junior classes. Mr. D. gave back papers. Previous to this, however, he passed out papers explaining corrections and some common mistakes which were to be avoided in the future. This "new" material, in the form of a handout, seemed to me to be a good way of using orientation (actually a form of review—much of the material on the sheets was old.)

*****

My lesson went much better. No interruption. I stuck closer to my time limit. My motivating sentence went well—it got a lot of response. It was a good introduction—got kids involved because they could correct the teacher's work. Terrance was so slow. I had to go on even though he was behind because most of the class was done and getting fidgety. Solution? I could work with him later. Yes—during extra time when they do seatwork. But he is behind in almost all of his work.

Mrs. A. had them read a story in reading. She introduced the lesson with the discussion on people's names in different languages. She began with the kids' experiences with other names. (Yura told some Spanish names) and then steered it around to Indian names (the story is about Indians.) So there was a clear purpose to the introduction. It got the students interested in the story, prepared them by focusing their attention and gave a preview of the story, somewhat.

*****

I like to give oral drill problems to begin math class. The kids like it too. It gets them thinking and practices basic facts and listening skills.

*****

In vocabulary section today, I made myself aware of my own use of set induction. Orientation: To begin my lesson, I held up a copy of Roget's Thesaurus and simply asked "Who can tell me what this is?" For some it was a review—it was a good springboard for moving into explanation of its use, as well as the rest of my material.

*****

This was the first period I was very happy with—interesting discussion evolved with regard to women's rights/suffrage, etc. For the first time, I felt I reached a proper balance between concentrating on my material and concentrating on my students. As a result, I controlled the discussion and, I felt, had some success in having the kids teach themselves/each other through their own comments on the subject and on the words.

*****

Mr. D. used a diagram (sense variation as stimulus variation) today in teaching an introduction to Milton's "Paradise Lost". I found it interesting to see how the lesson was structured around the formation/construction of the diagram—as it grew so the lesson expanded into its full form; it was a nice parallel structure, I thought.

*****

Attempts are made frequently, I feel, by Mr. D. and myself, to keep learning as student-centered as possible. For example, as a form of stimulus variation, the Juniors were today divided into groups to study "Paradise Lost". The effectiveness of this tool will be revealed tomorrow when the students presented their findings. I'm quite sure it helped students recoup some lost energy; hopefully, they put that energy to good use.

*****

Today I was very conscious of how I was closing my lessons. At the end of all my reading groups we reviewed the vocabulary words that we started the group with. At the end of my phonics groups, I asked the students to recall the words containing the short vowel studied today. At the end of every group (especially math), I find it necessary to review and have the students verbalize what their assignment is. Therefore, the last thing they hear in the group is the first thing they are to do when they return to their seats.

*****

I am still amazed at how easily Mrs. H. makes everything look. I know that with time I will make things look as smoothe and as polished. Student teaching is excellent. Being able to learn, to do it, to learn, and do it again is a great way to become a great teacher. I need that patience though because at times I wish I were doing more or feeling more comfortable when these uneasy times come. It takes time. It is good to walk down the hall and be recognized as a teacher by other teachers and students. Mrs. H. says it has to do with my presence.

Further References

Cooper, James M. et. al. Classroom Teaching Skills, 2nd ed. Lexington, Massachusetts: D. C. Heath and Company, 1982.

Gagne, Robert M. and Biggs, Leslie J. Principles of Instructional Design, 2nd ed. Chicago: Holt, Rinehart and Winston, 1979.

Gazda, George M. et. al. Human Relations Development. Boston: Allyn and Bacon, 1977.

Jacobsen, David, Paul Eggen, Donald Kauchak, et. al. Methods for Teaching: A Skills Approach, 2nd ed. Columbus, Ohio: Charles E. Merrill Publishing Company, 1985.

Jersild, Arthur T. When Teachers Face Themselves. New York: Teachers College Press, 1955.

Joyce, Bruce R., Clark C. Brown and Lucy Peak, editors. Flexibility in Teaching: An Excursion into the Nature of Teaching and Training. New York: Longman, 1981.

6 Presenting the Lesson

INTERACTION ACTIVITY: Communicating

Objective
To examine messages sent and determine if the same message is received.

To be concerned about getting things said is to focus on only part of the communication process. Total communication occurs when the message sent is the message received. Seeing behaviors and hearing responses which match the content of the message assures the sender that communciation is occurring. The receiver contributes to the communication process through paraphrasing and responding in other ways to what was heard.

Early in your teacher training you learned that the ability to communicate is among the skills essential to teaching. This interaction activity demonstrates different types of communication and refers to these different types as they apply to classroom teaching. Caught up with the content of an instructional activity you may be unaware of the quizzical expression on the faces of students, of the inaccurate information written about the assignment and of the learner who heard the first of three directions. On the other hand, because of extensive student questions and explanations, instructional tasks are delayed in starting.

Directions and Procedures

Leader: [Prior to calling the group together, select one member who is willing to direct this One-way and Two-way Communication Activity. The leader gives a picture of the diagram to the person describing the drawing to the group. Turn to Appendix A in the back of the book for diagrams needed in this activity. All group members are given two blank sheets of paper and asked to be seated so that the papers are not visible to others in the group. For the first part of this activity the director cannot be seen but can be heard by all.]

Leader: (Name) has agreed to direct you in this activity. Although you cannot see him/her, _____ will communicate verbally with you telling you what to draw on the paper before you. Do not talk, use sounds or communicate in any way while the directions are being given. Noises could distract others and interrupt their concentration. Follow, as carefully as you can, all directions given.

[The leader writes down the beginning and ending time for both the One-Way and Two-Way Activities. After the directions for the first activity are completed, the papers are collected and graded while the second activity is conducted. One point is given for each correct figure. At the same time the leader observes the behaviors of individuals within the group during both drawing exercises in order to make general reference to these during the discussion period.]

Leader: For the second activity, the director stands in front of the group. S/he, again, verbally describes the task. You may ask as many questions as you wish. The director can give as many verbal responses as you request.

[Following the completion of the second activity, comparisons are made between the time required for the two tasks. Participants share their perceptions of the following:]

Discussion Questions

Leader: A. With which method for receiving directions were you more comfortable?
B. To what extent was the other method more tense? Why?
C. With which method did you score higher?

[In addition to pointing out likenesses and differences in the group response the leader may describe specific behaviors of participants and ask reasons for such actions.]

Leader: A. Think about the two processes. Which process more nearly resembles the kind of communication you prefer if you are a participant?

B. Are there ever times when as teacher one-way communication should be used? Think of examples.

C. What are some examples of two-way communication being used in the classroom? Name some advantages.

SKILL ACTIVITY: **Lesson Presentation**

Objectives

To use procedures which get learners initially involved with instruction.

To provide opportunities for learner participation.

To maintain learner involvement through reinforcement techniques.

To combine and reiterate major points of the lesson presented.

Lesson presentation skills are essential to the learning process. You will continue to develop and practice these skills throughout your teaching. Using the following questions you will note your demonstrated competence and progress in using the introduction, variation of reinforcement and closure techniques.

1. Relate an introductory exercise you observed or used which kept the students motivated and involved with the content being presented. Tell how voice, audio visual or instructional aids, mental drill and lesson review were used in acquiring the learners attention.
2. Share in what ways the introductory activity was used later in the lesson to: (a) elicit further information, (b) make applications and/or, (c) make comparisons.
3. What types of drill, repetition, review, emphasis using voice or chalkboard were used in lessons? Which techniques did you consider effective in attaining the objectives set forth?
4. What methods were used in helping learners to retain material presented?
5. How did you emphasize the key points of your lesson?
6. During which part of the lesson was a summary or review used?

*****

Assignment (Using Questioning Techniques)

Skillful questioning techniques increase opportunities for learning in classroom instruction. John Dewey considered the questioning process as the very core of teaching. Formulating questions to stimulate thinking and appropriate response demands an understanding of the cognitive levels of development classified in Bloom's Taxonomy. Review these cognitive levels with some examples of questions in each of these levels listed below:

Levels of Cognitive Development and Examples of Questions

Level 1: Knowledge (recalls or recognizes information)
Ex: - What is closure?
- List the major steps used in solving a math problem.
Level 2: Comprehension (understands or knows what is being communicated)
Ex. - Discuss some differences between the cultures of India with the United States.
- Compare the Republican and Democratic platforms.
Level 3: Application (transfers learning from one context to another independently)
Ex. - Study the picture on page _____. Indicate what you would do to determine in what country this picture was taken.
Ex. - Mrs. Bell is purchasing a new home. She needs linoleum for her 20' x 20' kitchen. How much linoleum will she need to purchase? At $12 per square foot, what is her total cost?

Level 4: Analysis (breaks down a problem into parts and forms)
   Ex. - After completing the science experiment, what do you conclude is the name of the gas in the unlabeled test tube?
   - What information can you use to support the statement: President Lincoln was a friend to the slaves?

Level 5: Synthesis (putting together elements to form a creative whole)
   Ex. - Create a new instructional acitivity for a listening skill.
   - How can we raise money for the Crusade for Exceptional Children?

Level 6: Evaluation (makes value judgements using specific criteria)
   Ex. - Which of these pictures do you like best?
   - Do you think nuclear disarmament will lead to peace?

1. Test your ability to classify questions by selecting one question in each level from an instructors manual or learners text:

   Subject Area _____ Grade Level _____

   Knowledge _____

   _____

   Comprehension _____

   _____

   Application _____

   _____

   Analysis _____

   _____

   Synthesis _____

   _____

   Evaluation _____

   _____

2. Log the levels and the effectiveness of the questions asked in classes you observed or taught this week.

   Class _____ Date _____ Teacher_____

   Question_____

   Level_____ In what ways was it effective? _____

   _____

   _____

   Class _____ Date _____ Teacher_____

   Question _____

   Level_____ In what ways was it effective? _____

   _____

   _____

Class _____ Date _____ Teacher_____

Question _____

Level_____ In what ways was it effective? _____

_____

_____

Class_____ Date _____ Teacher_____

Question_____

Level_____ In what ways was it effective? _____

_____

_____

3. Give examples of learner initiated questions and your reaction to the teacher's response to the questions. (You may be the teacher!)

Student Question _____

Teacher Response _____

_____

Personal Reaction _____

_____

_____

Student Question _____

Teacher Response _____

_____

Personal Reaction _____

_____

_____

Student Question _____

Teacher Response _____

_____

Personal Reaction _____

_____

_____

Log Excerpts (Using Questioning Techniques)

Today I taught the freshman a section from grammar (prepositional phrases). —A million thoughts ran into my mind while I was teaching—enough to significantly distract my mind from the material I really wanted to cover. As a result, I probably was not as coherent as I perhaps could have been—I'm afraid I zeroed in a little too much on the students (eg., looking at them, trying to think of names, being close and attentive to them), and probably did not cover the material as effectively as I could have (eg., I found myself frequently referring to my notes—more than I should have; it really broke the rhythm of my lesson). Mr. D. also pointed out that I probably allowed too much time for the quiz I gave. The quizzes have, to some degree, reflected the prblems with my lesson (eg., some kids didn't follow directions, others made mistakes they should not have made). It will probably be a good idea to review the quizzes and re-cover some of the material.

*****

I taught large class and the smaller reading group. In the smaller group, it was easier to ask questions that required the student to think, apply, synthesize and evaluate. There was more time—I could give more individuals my attention and give them time to think. In large group such as in math when I taught the whole class, you have to keep things moving or else you lose the attention of half your class. In small groups, there is a narrower range of ability and your nearness holds their attention. Would be nice to have only 8 or 9 or 15 in class all day like we have for reading.

*****

I went over "Sounds and Patterns" in their spellers with the class . . . I felt comfortable in front of them. I walked around, checked answers and explained to a few individuals. One question was not very clear. I had to explain it myself. It's hard to think of different ways to present a question so that everyone can understand. I took too long—I let them have too much time to answer the questions. It's a fine line between giving them enough time and giving them too much time.

*****

I now need to focus in on students who don't always contribute orally. Some are good students and are standing well in class. Others, however, are not doing as well—perhaps through oral response I can find out why. (Failure warning cards go out next week.) In any case, I should know something about each student; getting them to talk is one way of doing this.

*****

This morning I was able to "wrap" things up in a reasonably tidy package—i.e., I got lucky! In the junior classes, on the other hand, I still have the tendency to get bogged down a little and never seem able to cover everything that I'd like to be able to. Generally, these kids ask perceptive questions which lead to more perceptive questions which make us run out of time. I don't feel that we ever waste time; we simply don't cover all the material I've planned. Tough decisions to make!

*****

In looking at the questions I have been asking in my reading groups this week, I noticed that there are a lot of inferential questions as well as literal questions, questions which require them to think of a cause and effect. Also I asked questions which would get them to begin thinking about distinguishing between things that are real and fantasy. Yesterday, besides asking questions such as these, we did an activity which required them to recall facts about the story and then to make guesses about the animals based on the facts.

*****

Last night, I prepared my reading lesson plan with types of questions specifically in mind. I tried to ask at least one each of Bloom's Taxonomy. Some kinds are easy to think of—recall, comprehension. Others, such as analysis and synthesis, are hard to think of. I realize I do not need to ask every kind during each lesson, as long as I keep them in mind and give the kids ample exposure to the different thought processes over the semester.

Ms. C. is now going over the boardwork with the first group of students. She is going to go over the rhyming words with them. Her questioning is very concise and step by step! She takes the students very precisely from one step to another.

*****

Mrs. A. followed up the TV program by helping the class write a limerick. She gave the topic of consumer education because of a visitor coming next week to observe (and possibly speak to the kids) about how consumer ed is incorporated into the classroom. She gave the first line and the kids offered the next ones. She questioned them so that they evaluated their ideas. "Does that line fit our pattern? Does it make sense? Could it be improved?" She used her bulletin board display to explain what consumer and consumer education is.

Further References

Bloom, Benjamin, editor. Taxonomy of Educational Objectives, Handbook I: Cognitive Domain. New York: David McKay, 1956.

Gagne, Robert M. and Leslie J. Briggs. Principles of Instructional Design. New York: Holt, Rinehart and Winston, 1979.

Gillin, Caroline T., Marcella L. Kipilka, Virginia M. Rogers, et. al. Questioneze. Columbus, Ohio: Charles E. Merrill Publishing Company, 1972.

Hunkins, Francis P. Questioning Strategies and Techniques. Boston: Allyn and Bacon, 1973.

_____. Involving Students in Questioning. Boston: Allyn and Bacon, 1976.

Hyman, Ronald T. Strategic Questioning. Englewood Cliffs, New Jersey: Prentice-Hall, 1979.

Sadker, Myra and David Sadker. "Questioning Skills." In James M. Cooper, general editor. Classroom Teaching Skills, 2nd. ed. Lexington, Massachusetts: D. C. Heath and Company, 1982.

Sanders, Norris M. Classroom Questions: What Kinds? New York: Harper and Row Publishing Company, 1966.

7 Using Questioning Techniques

INTERACTION ACTIVITY: Building Confidence

Objective
To recall a personal talent or an acquired teaching skill successfully applied in the classroom.

When was the last time you deliberately thought about a teaching technique you successfully used with learners? Have you taken notice of at least one ability or talent with which you were gifted? In straining to attain new goals, you may fail to acknowledge what has been accomplished. Reflecting on the past, and recalling abilities and talents builds self confidence for facing new challenges. Only after accomplishing established goals are some individuals convinced that they have the ability to succeed.

Striving to become an effective teacher is an extensive process. You are familiar with the research describing characteristics of effective teachers. Pondering and practicing behaviors congruent with these characteristics is the principle thrust of the activities assigned beginning teachers. In the Interaction and Skill Activities, you are asked to concentrate on some trait of the competent person and to recall an ability essential to effective teaching. Since awareness precedes the integration of cognitive understanding into personal behavior, you need to be patient with yourself and allow this transfer to occur. The practice of self acceptance and patience during this time mirrors the degree which you demonstrate acceptance toward others.

Directions and Procedures

[The **Leader** sets the tone by directing the group into a suitable physical arrangement.]

Leader: Deliberately distance yourself from the classroom setting and recall the importance of giving children and youth positive, verbal reinforcement. How important is it that learners believe in themselves, feel adequate, experience a sense of success. If as teacher you hold up mirrors reflecting positive images to students, you need to entertain good feelings towards yourself. Think back over the past days to one time when you realized success in some small event or activity which you can begin describing with the words, "I felt proud of myself . . ." Focus on the ability or talent which enables you to accomplish well some teacher task. Take a few minutes to reflect on an event which you can describe in this way.

[Allow 2-4 minutes of quiet time.]

Leader: Recognizing your own talents and abilities and directly telling others about them generally is done only with family and friends. You may feel awkward describing a competent performance and crediting it to your own talent. Realize that you are not alone with that feeling. In this group setting you are encouraged to risk to the greatest extent possible telling your partner about the demonstrated ability for which you felt proud. As the listener, be attentive to the expression in the voice and eyes as well as the emotion-expressing words.

[Allow 5-6 minutes and then call together the total group.]

Discussion Questions

Leader: A. How did you feel while another described his/her abilities?
B. Can you comment on your feelings while sharing your talents.
C. How often do you participate in an activity somewhat like this one?
D. How can you apply this interaction activity to other teacher responsibilities?

SKILL ACTIVITY: **Questioning**

Objectives
To observe, formulate and use classroom questions on all six levels of Bloom's <u>Taxonomy</u>.
To observe and reinforce learner questions throughout instruction.

   Questions are crucial to meaningful involvement in the teaching learning process. You need to be an effective model as a good questioner. The design and manner in which you phrase your questions influence the quality of the learner's response. You have opportunities to observe the types of questions used and the effect these questions have on learning in the classroom. Becoming question conscious may lead you as teacher to improve your questioning skill and create an effective learning environment.

1.   Cite examples of student questions. Were these questions used by the teacher to develop a topic? How were students stimulated to further explore the topic?

Student Question _____

Teacher Response _____

_____

_____

Comments _____

_____

_____

_____

Student Question _____

Teacher Response _____

_____

_____

Comments _____

_____

_____

_____

Student Question _____

Teacher Response _____

_____

_____

Comments _____

_____

2. Share examples of oral and written questions observed or used in your classes. What effect did the questions you selected have on student learning? While others are sharing questions you may use the following chart for keeping record of the variety of examples.

	ORAL	WRITTEN	Questions	KNOWLEDGE	COMPREHENSION	APPLICATION	ANALYSIS	SYNTHESIS	EVALUATION
1.									
2.									
3.									
4.									
5.									
6.									
7.									
8.									
9.									
10.									

Assignment (Teaching Concepts)

You are learning the importance of basic concept structure to the teaching learning process in planning and presenting lessons for your classes each day. Since all of the content areas are built around concepts it is important that in planning your lesson you are able to:

1. name or label the concept
2. define the concept
3. give the basic characteristics associated with the concept
4. list some examples and nonexamples of the concept
5. develop questions which elicit further examples or emphasize relationships with other concepts
6. select the most effective technique (AV equipment, written or oral questions) presenting examples and nonexample of concepts
7. determine what level of concept understanding you expect of your students and how you will measure the learning outcome.

Examine learner texts noting concepts and concept development this week. Log how concepts were sequentially developed in at least three classes using the following outline:

subject area _____

concept _____

definition _____

_____

basic characteristics _____

_____

examples _____

nonexamples _____

questions used (opening, clarifying, summarizing, etc.) _____

_____

_____

_____

_____

_____

technique (media used) _____

_____

evaluation _____

_____

subject area _____

concept _____

definition _____

_____

basic characteristics _____

_____

examples _____

nonexamples _____

questions used (opening, clarifying, summarizing, etc.)_____

_____

_____

_____

_____

subject area _____

concept _____

definition _____

_____

basic characteristics _____

_____

examples _____

nonexamples _____

questions used (opening, clarifying, summarizing, etc.)_____

_____

_____

_____

_____

Log Excerpts (Teaching Concepts)

For math, they discussed budgets. She asked them to think of expenses (synthesis). They looked up terms (recall and application) that deal with consumer ed (necessity, luxury, etc.). They write in their best handwriting; they read directions. This one lesson combines almost every subject plus the kids learn about consumer ed. It's great. Has their interest, is motivating and is teaching them many needed life skills often neglected.

*****

Today in the Sociology classes we reviewed for the test tomorrow. Before that, however, we did go over a concept. The concept was one of anomie. Anomie is a sociological term that refers to a condition in which there are no rules . . . it is a state of normlessness. Concept clusters dealt with such topics as deviance, labeling and roles.

Mrs. H. does not rely on using the board too much. Instead, she stimulates discussion and promotes learning by casually citing what she wants to teach from the text. What I feel are good examples are used to reinforce the concept. In order to reinforce the concept, the students are usually assigned some type of work. This involves doing either seat work or group work. I can see how seniors need less reinforcement than the freshman. The freshman seem to require a lot more redefining and explaining. Creative examples can be pulled from the seniors much more easily. The senior text deals with more abstract ideas, also. Concept teaching seems to be more easily done to know certain basic terms and vocabulary in order to be participating citizens.

*****

In math the fifth grade is continuing their concept of LCM. This is a hard concept for them and they're doing many reinforcing activities and exercises.

In English today the concept was the sentence. There was a cluster consisting of different types of sentences (compound, declarative, questioning, exclamation).

TO EXPAND:
What is a sentence? What are the two parts?
What does the subject tell us?
What does a predicate tell us?

She had students write a sentence and diagram on the board. (This was good, except I would have had the students in their seats to write the sentences while the others wrote at the board.)

*****

The fifth grade science concept was fossils today. We first talked about the various kinds and they then showed the ones they had brought to share. As they shared them, they used a copy of various types of fossils to identify the ones they brought.

*****

Miss B. is teaching the students in the Floats group how to read a graph by asking them what different things on the graph mean (she has drawn it on the board). This is a valuable skill. I don't think we were ever taught to do this in school and I still have trouble figuring out graphs and charts.

*****

My reading lesson uses a variety of questions. They had to synthesize or pull together threads and write a paragraph on the Pavia character who was not developed in the story. They applied the concept of the paragraph by writing one. They comprehended the material—had to place a checkmark beside the trait that belonged to a character after rereading a passage.

*****

Mr. D.'s approach was one of lecture, discuss, illustrate, work alone. My approach was one of introduce, use overhead to elicit response, probe, discuss, work alone/together. I'm learning very quickly that a multi-sense, multi-level, multi-media approach to teaching concepts is best. It not only frees me from the task of talking for fifty minutes, but also allows the student some break. I don't want to be talked at for lengths of time without the chance to contribute. Concept teaching frees the student and teacher. Page to page learning can be very tedious and boring.

*****

My reading lesson went very well, I think. The hardest skill for them was, of course, the part where they had to distinguish between fact and opinion (guesses). They did very, very well. I didn't think they would be able to do as well as they did until after I started the lesson. Then I realized that they are very quick at inferring so I made the task a little bit harder by demanding a little more thinking from them. They participated much better today, too!

Further References

Bruner, Jerome, Jacqueline J. Goodnow and George A. Austin. A Study of Thinking. New York: John Wiley, 1977.

Gagne, Robert M. and Leslie J. Briggs. Principles of Instructional Design. New York: Holt, Rinehart and Winston, 1979.

Jacobsen, David, Paul Eggen, Donald Kauchak, et. al. Methods for Teaching: A Skills Approach, 2nd ed. Columbus, Ohio: Charles E. Merrill Publishing Company, 1985.

Jarolimek, John and Clifford Foster. Teaching and Learning in the Elementary School, 2nd ed. New York: Macmillan Publishing Company, Incorporated, 1981.

Joyce, Bruce and Marsh Weil. Models of Teaching, 2nd ed. Englewood Cliffs, New Jersey: Prentice-Hall, 1980.

Klausmeier, Herbert J., Elizabeth Ghatala and Dorothy Frayer. Conceptual Learning and Development: A Cognitive View. New York: Academic Press, 1974.

Martorella, Peter H. "Teaching Concepts." In James M. Cooper, general editor. Classroom Teaching Skills, 2nd ed. Lexington, Massachusetts: D. C. Heath and Company, 1982.

Michaelis, John U. Social Studies for Children: A Guide to Basic Instruction, 8th ed. Englewood Cliffs, New Jersey: Prentice-Hall, 1985.

8 Teaching Concepts

INTERACTION ACTIVITY: **Becoming Competent**

Objective
To name one teaching skill developed or improved during the past weeks.

As the semester progresses, you advance from one level of involvement in the teacher-learning process to the next. Over a relatively short span of time you, the beginning teacher, are in process—are becoming. The teacher you become will be unique and greatly depend upon you and the goals you establish. A number of incidents contribute to this process of becoming. Modeling the supervising teacher's techniques, implementing recommendations and suggestions given you and reflecting on a student's successful learning in your class are all resources focusing attention on the teacher you intend to become.

In addition to classroom interaction the quality of participation in peer groups also contributes to your growth as person and as professional teacher. Active participation means that you examine the progress made in assuming the teacher role and that you examine self-established goals. Keep in mind that the group sharings enable you to realize that you are not alone with feelings of anxiety, elation, loneliness, inadequacy, etc. during this becoming process.

Directions and Procedures

[The leader sets the tone by directing the group into a suitable physical arrangement.]

Leader: This interaction activity, like that in Chapter 7, emphasizes maintaining a balanced perspective. You are more confident in planning, directing and anticipating learner responses. At times your teaching goes smoothly and effectively and you feel successful about your accomplishments. Yet, there are those times which are not satisfying. You look at the supervising teacher, at other teachers, and they seem to get more results in proportion to the effort expanded. Thinking about your teaching, you remember only those classes in which learners completed some of the activities and not all were attentive to directions and explanations you gave them.

Accurately perceiving student behavior is important for improving teacher skills; however, you feel disappointed and doubt that you will ever become competent. During such times you also need to deliberately recall accomplishments in your teaching. Take time to reflect on the skills you have used effectively. For example, think of set inductions which grabbed student attention and moved the class into the first phase of the lesson. How about the timing of activities? When planning, have you developed a sense of how long to spend on different parts of the class period? Recall how concerned you were about timing during the first week of classes. Think over the past few days and center on a time you felt most like teacher. Recall the skill or behavior you exhibited and for a few minutes relive the incident.

[Allow 2-4 minutes for reflection and then gain the group's attention.]

Leader: While reminding yourself of a particular skill acquired is reassuring, describing accomplishments by naming specific behaviors is useful for future exchanges with other teachers, administrators and parents. As a short range goal, isolating one skill reassures you that progress is being made. Since all in this group share some common goals, hearing the others describe their experiences can deepen your self-understanding. Select another group member and begin sharing your incident.

[Allow 5-6 minutes and then call together the total group.]

Discussion Questions

[If the group seems comfortable sharing as a total unit, omit the duo-setting and proceed to the large group. Remind the group to use words expressing feelings while describing a skill demonstrated. Some same phrases are the following: I felt confident . . . It seemed smooth and easy . . . I was in high spirits . . . Seeing the faces of the students thrilled me . . . I wanted to stand tall . . .]

Leader: A. How did the number of teaching behaviors you privately recalled compare with the number you shared with your partner?

B. In what way has this and other group interaction activities impacted your perspective as a beginning teacher?

C. How likely are you to tell yourself good things you recognize in your daily work?

SKILL ACTIVITY: **Concepts**

Objectives
To identify concepts in materials used with learners.
To describe various components for teaching concepts.

Concepts are basic ways of thinking and there are several models for organizing concept learning instruction. You have examined concepts and how they are developed in texts and other learner materials. Having experienced planning how to present concepts or observed concept teaching, exchange the information you gathered:

1. Give examples of concepts used in (a) learner texts and, (b) teacher plan and presentation.
2. Using plans from two consecutive lessons taught, i.e. math on Monday and Tuesday to the same group, examine and share the sequential development of the concept taught.
3. How does concept teaching expand thinking and inquiry in the students?

*****

Assignment (Selecting Teaching Materials and Equipment)

Selecting the appropriate materials and equipment for instructional use is a skill you will want to continually develop and process. Examine the library offerings for texts, trade books, films, filmstrips, recordings, computers, etc. Be attentive to the instructional materials and equipment you see or use within the classroom.

1. Observe uses of AV equipment in yours or other classes.

Who uses the equipment?_____

For whom is it used?_____

When is it used? (i.e.) motivation, factual input_____

_____

Comments_____

_____

_____

_____

2. Examine your curriculum guides for subject matter and/or grade level. Notice and comment on the following:

Subject matter _____

Grade level _____

Objectives _____

_____

_____

_____

_____

Scope and sequence _____

_____

_____

_____

_____

_____

_____

_____

_____

Suggested supplementary materials _____

_____

_____

_____

_____

_____

_____

_____

_____

_____

_____

_____

_____

_____

_____

_____

3. Check your mastery of the following materials/equipment in the appropriate box:

	Observer	Assistant	Expert
Attendance Book			
Grade Book			
Overhead Projector			
Duplicating Machine			
Film/Filmstrip Projector			
Computer			

Log Excerpts (Selecting Teaching Materials and Equipment)

Ms. A. also asked the class this morning if they had heard of the incident in Egypt. This was good because it showed them it was important to keep up with the news. Egypt was pointed out on the map also. Ms. A. said she was going to "hire" a news reporter to inform the class each morning of world and local news. She said she'd be taking applications.

*****

The concept of "how a bill becomes law" is not an easy one for freshman to understand or get interested in. As an aid in learning and interest-building, we showed a filmstrip that dealt in detail with how a bill becomes law. It uses many different kinds of drawings, charts, and pictures to illustrate the process. Quotations from congressmen are used to highlight the material.

As a further aid to the student, we stopped the filmstrip often at a point in which we wanted. At this time we told the student what important note to write down. We also wrote a brief note on the board pertaining to the item we wanted them to pay attention to. This was a multi-faceted approach to getting across the concept. We relied on the filmstrip, we stopped and stressed important points, the students made note of these in their notebook, we also wrote these notes on the board—a many tiered approach. Tomorrow we'll also make a drawing of the process that the students can copy down in their notebooks.

*****

Ms. B. utilizes everything. She uses each of her bulletin boards to teach. For example, she used many creative writing bulletin board to teach the six kinds of questions (who, what, etc.). She uses one bulletin board to teach current events, one to teach consumer ed, and so on. Each is a visual aid that reinforces, aids by summarizing information, is attractive as a display and is a constant reminder to students.

Mrs. G. used puppets today. "Old Timer" and a witch. It was great. She used them to review Columbus, etc. Also said Old Timer would watch and take down names of those who are bad. Also that he wanted good reports. Kids loved it! I did too.

*****

I used filmstrip in science on digestive system. The first time I had used a projector of this kind in the class. I was prepared for it beforehand. While the kids were working quietly, I asked Mrs. A. to show me how to use it so I wouldn't have to fool around and waste time when I needed it. When I did use it, I asked Melanie to run the projector. She did a good job (and I let her know). By letting her do it, I could concentrate on the information in the film—was a review and brushup for me. Plus it gave me a better idea of how much to present to these fifth graders. I sat in an empty desk behind Mike. This kept everyone quiet and eyes on the film. I prepared them for the film by reviewing the chart and discussing what we needed to find out. At one point, I stopped the film so they could copy down needed information. The film was followed up by discussing the system and finishing the chart.

*****

Using the overhead is more time efficient when giving dictation. I can turn it off, write the sentence and turn it on when the kids are done. If you write the sentence on the board, you have to wait till all are done so no one will copy. This wastes time. Plus it is an excellent model for handwriting. When you write on the board, it's hard for the kids to see your motions plus you are working with chalk and so it's different from the kids' experiences with the pencil. It's the same experience when you use the pen on the overhead and they can see exactly the way the letter is made.

*****

Another visual/tactile aid I have used this week was a poster of a clover. On the clover were several "cl" words. The children took the marker (they get so excited about this) and circled the cluster in each "cl" word. Today I am using a grab bag (box actually) which contains different objects for the children to feel and describe.

*****

For math today, Mrs. A. taught addition and conversion of measurements. She used the overhead. She wrote problems and then picked a child to come up and solve it on the overhead. The kids were motivated—want to write on the overhead. She used a chart. Helps kids to be more organized and is less easy to mess up. Using the overhead also helps us to see how a child thinks when he solves problems and how he forms his numerals. We don't always have time to check everyone for these things when they work problems on paper. This is a way to spot check.

Further References

Brown, James W., Richard B. Lewis, and Fred F. Harcleroad. AV Instruction: Materials and Methods, 5th ed. New York: McGraw-Hill, 1977.

Foster, Harold M. The New Literacy: The Language of Film and Television. Urbana, Illinois. National Council of Teachers of English, 1979.

Gerlach, V. L. and D. P. Ely. Teaching and Media, A Systematic Approach, 2nd ed. Englewood Cliffs, New Jersey: Prentice-Hall, 1980.

Joyce, Bruce and Marsha Weil. Models of Teaching, 2nd ed. Englewood Cliffs, New Jersey: Prentice-Hall, 1980.

Minor, Edward O. and Harvey R. Frye. Techniques for Producing Visual Instructional Media, 3rd ed. New York: McGraw-Hill, 1978.

Schramm, W. L. Big Media, Little Media: Tools and Technologies for Instruction. Beverly Hills: Sage Publications, 1977.

Wittich, W. A. and C. F. Schuller. Instructional Technology: It's Nature and Use, 6th ed. New York: Harper and Row, 1979.

9 Selecting Teaching Materials and Equipment

INTERACTION ACTIVITY: Taking Stock

Objective
To compare self awareness and perception of the teaching role at this time with those stated earlier.

Throughout the past weeks many changes involving you have taken place. You are aware of differences in the degree of importance you attach to certain aspects of teaching. The daily classroom routine, focusing on certain theories and practicing specific skills have influenced your view of the teacher you are becoming. You, perhaps, have expanded your perceptions of the teaching role.

This interaction activity asks you once again to pause and consider questions about your expectations of the teacher role. Although you answered these same questions some weeks ago, your new and evolving role causes rapid changes in your perceptions to occur. List specific strengths and expectations you have of yourself as teacher at this time. Do not consult your earlier responses to these questions.

Directions and Procedures

[The leader directs the group into an appropriate physical arrangement.]

Leader: Here are 3 questions. You may remember seeing these questions some weeks ago; however, do not think about the responses you gave at that time. Be spontaneous in your comments, writing phrases and words which come first to mind after reading the question. You are the only person who will be seeing what you write.

[Display the 3 questions or use the space provided in the text. Allow approximately 5 minutes for writing. Have available the individuals' envelopes containing the writing from the earlier group meeting. As participants finish writing, distribute envelopes and direct their review and comparison of responses.]

1. What aspect of the teaching role do you see as most important?

   _____

   _____

   _____

2. What is the most difficult aspect of the teaching role as you perceive it at this time?

   _____

   _____

   _____

3. What do you as beginning teacher bring to the school and classroom?

   _____

   _____

   _____

Discussion Questions

Leader: Now, take each question and compare the responses you wrote today with that written some weeks ago. After reading the responses, reflect on the likenesses and differences between the two:

A. In what ways are today's comments like those written earlier in the teaching experience?
B. To what extent do the earlier responses indicate that the anticipated difficulties were actually realized?
C. Which teacher responsibilities and expectations were easier to assume? Why?

SKILL ACTIVITY: **Educational Materials Utilization**

Objectives

To select appropriate educational materials and equipment suitable for instruction.
To prepare instructional materials providing for differences in learning styles.

All types of instructional materials are essential to a well rounded curriculum program. Instructional materials including educational technology offer teachers and students exciting and motivational means of involvement and enthusiasm for learning. You have been challenged to examine, select and use a variety of materials and audio visuals suited for varied student capabilities. Using the information gathered, respond to the following questions:

1. To what extent does the instruction in your class satisfy the objectives of the Curriculum Guide for your subject area or department? Give examples.
2. At what time this week, during the lesson presentation, was a picture, display, film, recording or any other audiovisual used? How did the audiovisual reinforce learning?
3. Are your students computer literate? To what extent are computers used within the curriculum?
4. Recall a film or TV program you have observed or used with students. Share the learner preparation and follow-up activity. Describe the extent these materials promoted learner interest and understanding.
5. To what extent do you suggest that instructional materials contribute to the development of visual literacy?

*****

Assignment (Focusing on Teacher Student Interaction)

You are successful as teacher to the degree that students acquire the learning you intended for them. Already, you realize that teacher behaviors effect the degree to which this occurs. You provide the structure wherein the efforts, interests and time of individual learners and groups on academic activities prevent disruptions.

Activities from earlier chapters emphasized sending clear verbal and nonverbal messages, using attending behaviors as listener and growing in self awareness. These are skills and characteristics teachers need in order to promote an academic learning environment and in building relationships with and among students. The assignment focuses on the number and kinds of interactions you have with students. You have the opportunity to self evaluate and to gain feedback from observations of your use of certain skills.

1. Tally the interaction between teacher and students during two classes of the same students this week. You may use the following seating chart adapting it to tally student interaction with the teacher or with other students during lesson presentations.

1	2	3	4	5
6	7	8	9	10
11	12	13	14	15
16	17	18	19	20
21	22	23	24	25
26	27	28	29	30
31	32	33	34	35

2. Log examples of verbal and written expressions you used this week to reinforce learners who demonstrate:

on task behavior _____

_____

_____

_____

consideration of others _____

_____

_____

_____

continuous progress toward a single goal_____

_____

_____

_____

following directions _____

_____

_____

_____

independent work habits _____

_____

_____

_____

_____

_____

_____

_____

_____

_____

_____

_____

_____

_____

3. Tally your supervising teacher's interaction behaviors or ask him/her to tally yours as you observe or are observed during two classes this week. You may discuss the results after the second class has been recorded on the chart provided.

Student Teacher

Tally the number of times you notice the following:

	Date	Date
Eye Contact ex. Looks at students while teaching them, Eye range includes all learners		
Facial Expression ex. Matches verbal expression, Pleasant, smiling, listening		
Posture ex. Alert and attentive to learner participants, confident		
Gestures ex. Nodding in agreement, shaking head in disagreement, Placing hand on shoulder Pointing to examples		
Voice ex. Clear, articulate, Changes inflection, volume and rate		
Position to Learner ex. Moves about the classroom to view all learners		

Log Excerpts (Focusing on Teacher Student Interaction)

Pam is always sick. She's very smart and keeps up but is missing a lot of school. She always has something wrong with her and will tell us. We haven't been playing along with her—we tell her to forget her pains and concentrate on work or play. This morning before school, she cried and wanted to go home. Mrs. A. brought her back to the classroom and gave her jobs to do. The thing to do is to keep a close eye on her. And call parents tonight (which Mrs. A. is going to do) and work with them on the problem—get more information on her problem and see how parents view it. From what I understand, mother is the same way so it's probably something Pam has learned to get attention. Mrs. A., by giving Pam morning jobs, is giving her attention but not by recognizing her "illnesses."

*****

I took them out for P.E. today. We played kickball. I was referee, encourager, congratulator and monitor in all. Sometimes you just have to laugh at all the arguments and ignore some of them. I let kids work some of them out themselves unless it came down to a shouting match between two teams.

*****

Ms. B. reinforced in more ways than I did. I say "good" a lot—maybe too much. It may be so common that it has no effect on the kids. I am getting better in giving verbal reinforcement in different ways but could improve quite a bit.

*****

I also still ask for someone to come to the board. I have had refusals too. Sometimes, I tell them to come if they refuse. Other times, I don't push it. It depends on the situation. But this would be avoided if I told them to do it in the first place. Will have less refusals. I'll try to work on it. It's hard. It seems questions like these slip out before I realize I could state it in a better way and achieve better results. I need to concentrate more on what I am going to say. So many things to think about!

*****

I taught vocabulary section today and the lesson went much better. The students seemed to be pretty involved by the time I finished, which, for me, is a good progression. Still, there was much I wish I would have done but didn't realize until I was in the middle of the lesson. For example, there were times when I probably should have elicited comments on some of the words which have gone beyond the mere book material I was covering. I did this some, but will do it a bit more often in the future. I had students write (spell) words on the board which really seemed to put them squarely into the flow—I like the technique and its results.

*****

It's funny but it seems that the children I have extreme difficulty with, Miss B. is extra patient with. And visa-versa. Some of the kids that absolutely drive her crazy, I have patience with. This is good for the kids in the classroom. But I worry about the kids in the classroom in the future. I really must watch my interactions with them.

. . . .

When a group has done well in the reading time, Ms. S. always tells them how well they did. This is so reinforcing for them! I need to do this more.

*****

There is a little girl in class—Mona. She is a little quiet mouse very hesitant, slow in her work although she has a knack for creative writing. But she has a temper—cross her and you'll get an "I'm sorry" or "Excuse me." It's pretty funny because it is so surprising when she gets feisty, yet she needs to learn to control her temper. Two days ago, a few boys laughed; she cried and cussed and said she was tired. Mrs. A. calmed her down and had planned on talking to her yesterday, but she was absent. Mrs. A. has talked with her mother, "Mona's been sick but does need to control her temper." She's back today and so far is doing OK. I like the way Mrs. A. handled it—calming her, letting her sit on the bean bag till she quit crying, moving her desk away from the boy who laughed and planning on talking to her next day after she had time to calm down even more and could think clearly. This would also give the teacher time to consider how to handle the talk and what expectations of improvement are realistic of this child.

My morning was so good. The kids were really cooperating well. I can tell that they really respect me and value my decisions. That feels good, of course.

*****

I love to kid with the children but sometimes I'm not sure how far to go. I guess I can just use my common sense about it. I just hope my common sense is accurate.

*****

Craig seemed to be doing fairly well. He is raising his hand eagerly to answer questions. Mrs. C. isn't giving him a lot of extra attention—is letting him settle in. This is good—he is already in the spotlight without being pointed out. She did use him a few times to reinforce. For example: "Craig is new, so for his benefit let's go over . . ." She started metric measurements today in math. He did fine.

*****

Eddie just lied and cheated openly to Ms. S. in the match race. Ms. S. really let him have it but then just when he seemed to be about to throw a tantrum, she kidded him about something. What an excellent way to handle it. She made her point without Eddie losing face. I'm afraid I forget to use humor with Eddie even though I've read how important humor is with angry children.

*****

The children are very talkative this week. I think it's because of the rainy weather added to the Halloween season. They are responding well to oral work and discussion lessons even though we're having some trouble keeping them on task in quiet work.

*****

I am particularly pleased with the first period class. The discussion was well-ordered with people listening to one another. Several non-contributing students spoke up. The fourth period discussion was less thrilling. Students were not as interested. I resorted to calling on students for response—they responded beautifully when I did. I hope to make use of this in the future.

*****

Ms. A. is acting very low key today because she knows all the kids are hyped up for Halloween. This is very effective. She is using lots of walking around the room and touching the children on the shoulder to calm them.

*****

Today Ms. C. announced that our class won the monthly award for cafeteria behavior for October. I think they will all get a treat from the cafeteria. The class who has the most months at the end will get an extra field trip. The kids are really excited but Ms. C. emphasized that they need to be especially good this month so they'll be able to get the trip.

*****

We're going to start having a different order of subjects starting today. She's doing this to show me how the classroom would work if I were not in the room and she had to handle the entire class. This will be good, especially so I can see how I will handle my own classroom without someone to help me.

61

Further References

Brophy, Jere E. and Carolyn M. Evertson. Student Characteristics and Teaching. New York: Longman, 1981.

Burke, J. Bruce. "Communicating with Students". In Introduction to Education. Donald C. Orlosky. Columbus, Ohio: Charles E. Merrill Publishing Company, 1982, pp. 250-289.

Cooper, James M., Peter H. Martorella and Greta D. Moring Dershimer, et. al. Classroom Teaching Skills, 2nd ed. Lexington, Massachusetts: D. C. Heath and Company, 1982.

Ginott, Haim G. Teacher and Child: A Book for Parents and Teachers. New York: Macmillan Company, 1972.

Good, Thomas L. and Jere E. Brophy. Looking In Classrooms, 3rd. ed. New York: Harper & Row Publishers, 1984.

Gordon, Thomas with Noel Burch. T. E. T.: Teacher Effectiveness Training. New York: Peter H. Wyden Publishers, 1974.

Hamacheck, Don E. Encounters with the Self, 2nd ed. New York: Holt, Rinehart and Winston, 1978.

Hennings, Dorothy Grant. Mastering Classroom Communication: What Interaction Analysis Tells the Teacher. Santa Monica, California: Goodyear Publishing Company, 1975.

Hurt, H. Thomas, Michael D. Scott and James C. McCroskey. Communication in the Classroom. Reading Massachusetts: Addison-Wesley Publishing Company, 1978.

Jersild, Arthur T. When Teachers Face Themselves. New York: Teachers College Press, Columbia University, 1955.

Kash, Marilyn M. and Gary D. Borich. Teacher Behavior and Pupil Self-Concept. Reading, Massachusetts: Addison-Wesley Publishing Company, 1978.

Schmuck, Richard and Patricia A. Schmuck. Group Processes in the Classroom. Dubuque, Iowa: William C. Brown Company, 1979.

10 Focusing on Teacher Student Interaction

INTERACTION ACTIVITY: Modeling

Objective
To consider modeling behavior and to recall examples used to direct learners.

What do you expect of students in the classroom setting? What do you expect of yourself as teacher? How are expectations of students integrated with expectations of yourself as teacher? The willingness to look within yourself, to identify and accept what you find there, greatly affects what you do and what you say in your interaction with others.

Expecting others to act responsibly and to contribute positively to the learning environment is more likely to occur when you as teacher effectively communicate this. Modeling is one means of sending messages. These may be indirect and subtle, yet, deliberately and consistently demonstrated. Your manner of speaking and acting can be a form of modeling. Do you think of yourself as a role model for students? Sounds somewhat boastful? Your saying, "Class imitate me in . . ." seems a bit hokey? "I can't expect myself to carry through every resolution!" Actually, you as teacher are modeling in many ways during a single day.

Directions and Procedures

[The Leader directs the group into an appropriate setting for the activity.]

Leader: The interaction activity invites you to reflect on the type of teacher communication called modeling. Mentally distance yourself from the classroom activities and focus on a single class or group of students. You may recall one topic or event which you spoke to the class about their manner of speaking and treating others in the class or in the school. In reinforcing this message to the students, were there deliberate gestures and actions you are aware of using? Stop for a few minutes and reflect on the past few days; select one occasion when you said in some way to your students "Imitate me in . . ."

[After allowing 2-4 minutes of quiet time the leader directs the group to share their experience with another.]

Leader: As you have done in previous sessions move next to a person in the group with whom you have not recently shared. Describe an incident of modeling you did with students and any effects which you observed or wanted to see exhibited by students. Remember, also, that good listening is attending to the person speaking. You, furthermore, can use affective phrases and words which check out with the speaker if you received the intended message. For example you may respond to your partner something like this: ". . . felt all eyes upon you watching to see what you would do . . .
. . . weren't sure the shy student in the hall would talk with you . . .
. . . struggled for precise words while feeling angry inside . . .
. . . strained to keep from laughing while repeating information students needed for their notes . . ."

[Allow 5-6 minutes for sharing in dyads and then call together the total group.]

Discussion Questions

Leader: A. Why is it helpful for you to reflect upon personal motives in your silences, words and actions?
 B. As compared with your initial experience talking about yourself how comfortable are you now in sharing personal thoughts?
 C. How have insights gained in this setting applied to other aspects of teaching?
 D. In what ways are you more aware of using listening skills?

SKILL ACTIVITY: **Teacher Student Interaction**

Objectives
To identify interaction patterns between teacher and learners within the classroom setting.
To convey positive regard for students through varied verbal and written expressions.
To identify strengths and weaknesses in the individual's style of teaching behavior.

As you enter the classroom each day, you bring numerous feelings and experiences which significantly affect your behavior. The activities you performed this week, were designed to increase awareness of verbal and nonverbal behavior and how it affects the learning process. You also observed how you perceived the motivation which underlies the behavior of students in various settings. Reviewing entries written in the Log during the past few days provides a resource for the following:

1. Share with the group some examples of learner behavior:

    . . . learners listening to each other _____

    _____

    . . . working as a group on a joint project _____

    _____

    . . . learner response to mistakes made _____

    _____

2. You have identified a variety of verbal and written expressions you could use to reinforce learners. Share with another three to five positive reinforcers you used this week. What learner responses were evoked?
3. What means do you use in extending direction to a large group while working with a small group?
4. After examining the chart completed by your supervising teacher, list below ways you might improve your interaction with learners.

Behavior   Ideas for Improvement

_____

_____

_____

_____

_____

_____

_____

_____

Assignment (Managing the Classroom)

Not only beginning but also experienced teachers name discipline among the major teacher concerns. Knowing that you are not alone in your fear of establishing and maintaining academic engagement affords momentary comfort. There is no best list of discipline strategies guaranteeing success in every situation. Teachers who are effective in managing instruction and learner behavior, seem to have the following: (a) ability to relate interpersonally; (b) knowledge and acceptance of self and of the teacher they aspire to be: (c) preference for strategies consistent with a single philosophical base. Gaining these skills and characteristics began prior to beginning to teach and the process extends continuously. At this time reviewing the various strategies and examining what you observe and use, class by class and day after day are needed for strengthening the discipline component of teaching.

The interaction activities as well as the skill activities emphasize the importance of your perception of the teacher role. Accepting your role as one of authority, responsible for determining the management process, is an important primary understanding. Then, there are specific teacher expectations for learners which need consistent and periodic communication. In addition, you, as teacher, decide which strategies at any given time are most likely to encourage and sustain student engagement with learning tasks. If students are disruptive, you must select from yet another set of strategies. Adjusting to the role and employing strategies for specific situations take time and practice. The skill activities provide examples for recalling and applying techniques which encourage learner involvement; other techniques are intended to terminate disruptive behavior.

Techniques found in the skill activities are classified according to the following theories:

A. Fostering desirable behaviors; eliminating undesirable behaviors. These are most like behavioral modification approaches to managing the total class.
B. Controlling student behaviors. Techniques in which the teacher takes charge, enforces rules and follows through with consequences belong in this category.
C. Promoting interpersonal relationships among students and with the teacher. While establishing and maintaining a learning environment these techniques tend to encourage personal accountability and can strengthen self discipline within students.
D. Eliciting the support and authority of others. Techniques which elicit the endorsement of parents and/or school administrators may prevent or eliminate disruptive classroom behaviors.

1. If you were not present when class rules were established, talk with the supervising teacher about how and when rules were established.
    Is there a list of rules posted? _____ Yes _____ No
    Name those rules which are consistently enforced. How is this done?

    Rule _____

    How enforced _____

    _____

    _____

    _____

    Rule _____

    How enforced _____

    _____

    _____

    _____

2. Techniques used with the total group or individuals. Describe the effect of using the techniques with the group/individuals.

Discipline Techniques	No. of times used	Individual	Group	Effect on Individual Learner/Class Discipline
1. Ignores inappropriate behavior				
2. Rewards appropriate behavior				
3. Refers to another learner model ("I like the way . . . ")				
4. Assigns time out				
5. Assigns clean up area				
6. Student restores damages; pays equivalent money				
7. Withholds privileges				
8. Assigns extra work				
9. Sends student to principal				
10. Calls parent, solicits support				
11. Calls learner by name				
12. Moves close to student				
13. Switches off lights				
14. Terminates all activity: (silence)				
15. Places hand on shoulder-- behavior noticed while class continues				
16. Listens and encourages learner to express problems				
17. Encourages cooperation				
18. Student describes own behavior; states improved course of action				
19. Describes situation, expresses feelings, clarifies expectations				

3. Describe two incidents which challenged you to resolve a behavioral problem with a learner in class this week. What techniques did you use in resolving the problem? Why?

Problem 1: _____

_____

_____

_____

Techniques used: _____

Why? _____

Problem 2: _____

_____

_____

Techniques used: _____

Why? _____

_____

Log Excerpts (Managing the Classroom)

The techniques for classroom management we have discussed are becoming more evident to me. It is quite fun to experiment with them and see them work. I was, for example, having some problems with side conversations during class (not all of which were bad). Today I decided to present the problem, mention the times when they can converse (e.g. between classes, lunch, etc.), and present in a positive way my expectations for their behavior in my class--it all worked quite well! I was amazed and surprised, though I had no reason to be. Why wouldn't it work?

*****

Today, genuinely for the first time, I felt myself get angry at a student after a smart remark made about a homework assignment. I found the remark especially disrespectful, and it for some reason really got under my skin. Fortunately the incident occurred right as Mr. D. was beginning to take over the lesson. The kid knew I was angry from the long glare I gave him and caused no more problems for the remainder of class. In the meantime, I was able to cool down a bit and deal with the problem in what I thought was a rational way. (I took the kid aside and talked to him after class and explained why I was angry. He understaood immediately and things seemed to be cleared up rather quickly.) In any case, I'm sort of glad things happened as they did--I'm a little suspicious of anyone who never gets angry. When it happens again, hopefully I'll know what's happening and realize a little more quickly the appropriate action I should take. Mr. D. was very supportive.

*****

The student I had trouble with yesterday was unusually good, contributive and productive in class today. I tried to act as if his behavior was the normal, acceptable behavior in my class--in the end, I think he appreciated this.

*****

I am trying the same tactics with Eddie as we decided to try with Shannon. It is hard for me not to get angry with Eddie. He requires my most patience!!!

*****

I've been having P.E. each day with them. It's getting better for me. They are listening to each other and they have learned I don't reinforce name-calling or "nasty" remarks. I praise those who are good sports and who try their best.

*****

I decided to give Mike a second chance. I divided up the day so there isn't such a long stretch of time before reward is given. If good in morning, will reward at lunchtime. He suggested the sticker I took away from him yesterday. I agreed. Took a minute to think of reward for second half of day. He finally suggested I let the class play kickball (he loves it) during P.E. I agreed. I was satisfied--both rewards are his suggestions and are not something rest of class will resent. Plus we have made a contract--instead of me telling him what to do. God, please let it work!

Further References

Alschuler, Alfred S. School Discipline. New York: McGraw-Hill Company, 1980.

Charles, C.M. Building Classroom Discipline. New York: Longman, 1981.

Clarizio, Harvey F. Toward Positive Classroom Discipline. New York: John Wiley and Sons, 1980.

Curwin, Richard L. and Allen N. Mendler. Taking Charge in the Classroom. Reston, Virginia: Reston Publishing Company, 1983.

Dreikurs, Rudolf, and Pearl Cassel. Discipline Without Tears. New York: Hawthorn Books, 1972.

Duke, D.L. ed. Classroom Management. The Seventy-Eighth Yearbook of the National Society for the Study of Education. Chicago: University of Chicago Press, 1979.

Glasser, William. Schools Without Failure. New York: Harper and Row, 1969.

Gordon, Thomas. T.E.T. Teacher Effective Training. New York: David McKay, 1974.

Howard, Rose A. An Investigation of Discipline Techniques Used by Effective Teachers. Ann Arbor, Michigan: ERIC Document Reproduction Service, Ed 305, 301, 1979.

Kounin, Jacob S. Discipline and Group Management in Classroom. Atlanta: Holt, Rinehart and Winston, 1970.

Madsen, Charles H., Jr. and Clifton K. Madsen. Teaching Discipline: A Positive Approach for Educational Development. Boston: Allyn and Bacon, 1981.

Rinne, Carl H. ATTENTION The Fundamentals of Classroom Control. Columbus, Ohio: Charles E. Merrill Publishing Company, 1984.

Tanner, Laurel N. Classroom Discipline for Effective Teaching and Learning. Atlanta: Holt, Rinehart and Winston, 1978.

Walker, J.E. and T.M. Shea. Behavior Modification: A Practical Approach for Educators. St. Louis: The C.V. Mosby Company, 1980.

Wolfgang, C.H. and C.D. Slickman. Solving Discipline Problems: Strategies for Classroom Teachers. Boston: Allyn and Bacon, 1980.

11 Managing the Classroom
INTERACTION ACTIVITY: Cooperating and Coping

Objective
To emphasize self discipline needed in cooperative efforts and to note causes of stress.

Along with students, teachers work with other teachers, administrators, school personnel and parents. While directing the day-to-day operations within the total group, teachers are also expected to observe individual students engaged in learning tasks and to keep within a scheduled amount of time. Managing materials, schedules, individual and group needs and responding to unexpected situations during class time is demanding. For the beginning teacher responding to this broad array of demands can be stressful. Balancing the constraints on time and energy while maintaining a healthy perspective on less-than-perfect performance is vital in coping with expectations you and others have of you as a professional.

From your working in the school you have learned that being teacher includes not only you but other members of the profession as well. Much of your own success depends on your ability to work with others. Think back to the beginning days with this class. Recall some of the first responsibilities you assumed, some suggestions and comments given after your first teaching experiences. Even though you now have much greater instructional responsibility, you can recount numerous examples of depending upon others and times when they depend upon you. At the same time you are learning to cope with various parts of the teacher role, you can see the need for cooperation.

Directions and Procedures

[Materials needed for this are: (a) set of individual envelopes containing one or more geometric pieces from the five squares; (b) participant groups of five. Prior to meeting the leader has checked to see that all parts of each square is available in envelopes for the five-member groups. See Appendix B for illustrations of the completed squares. Appoint at least one observer for each group. Describe the function of the observer as one who sees that rules are kept by the group and watches the movements of each participant.]

Leader: This activity requires that you work together according to certain rules. Each member has a number of puzzle pieces in the envelope which has been distributed. Each of the five persons is to assemble a square of exactly the same size from puzzle pieces. All pieces in group must be used. No puzzle has pieces of the same shape as another. Although some may appear to be the same basic shape, they do not fit together within the regular geometric form. During the activity no person may speak to any other member nor may he/she indicate approval or disapproval at another member's efforts by any nonverbal means, facial expressions and gestures. No person may take a puzzle piece from another or signal in any way that he/she wants it. However, any group member may give one or more of his/her pieces to another person by placing the piece into the hand of the person to the right. Pieces may be received only from the left. You may help another group member form his/her square by circulating the pieces keeping aware of others needs while not neglecting your own project. When all members of a group have squares of equal size, raise your hand to signal that your goal is accomplished.

[After all groups have finished, ask observers for feedback. Then ask members of group to respond.]

Discussion Questions

Leader: A. Describe your feelings while you played the game. How did you feel toward yourself? Toward others?
  B. Were you able to act as observer and player at the same time--both constructing your own square and contributing pieces to other members?
  C. What caused the group to be tense?
  D. How possible was it to see a need which another had to recognize and yet remain silent, patient?
  E. Can you think of situations in the classroom setting which require that the teacher's attention be divided among three or more concerns?

SKILL ACTIVITY: **Managing the Classroom**

Objectives
To identify the discipline techniques observed and used.
To examine the theory supporting classroom practices.
To self assess behaviors contributing to effective discipline.

Just as instructional strategies occupy the major portion of this book, so also, their skillful application satisfy most classroom management concerns. Proficiency in managing behavior is important and frequently is intertwined with other teaching skills. Reviewing discipline strategies and examining those observed in the classroom provide time for strengthening skills in this specific area as you begin teaching.

Referring to the assignment sheets from the previous chapter and to your experiences with establishing and maintaining discipline respond to these questions:

1. To which of the class rules do you most often remind students? In reviewing for students the expected behavior what seems to motivate individuals and the group to cooperate and try harder?
2. Name the discipline techniques you most often use/observe and explain the theory which underlies these practices. (Techniques 1-8; Techniques 9-10; Techniques 11-14; Techniques 15-19.)
3. Which management techniques are you attempting to acquire and how do you see them contributing to the teaching learning process?
4. With what aspect of discipline are you now more confident than you were some weeks ago?
5. Discuss the effects of the following instructional components on the learning environment: lesson plans, pacing, directions given to learner, assignments.

*****

Assignment (Making Assignments)

Planning effectively for learner achievement requires verbal and written responses from the learner. The inital lesson presentation plan might include written or verbal response to questions asked. Learners may be assigned a number of math problems to be completed, pages to be read in preparation for discussion, a science experiment, completion of creative writing activity, a page from the skill or activity book or any variety of activities for different purposes. Purposes might be any of the following: preparation for individual response in class or for group discussion, follow-up application and/or reinforcement of concept taught, creative challenge to further learner thinking or discovery, and enrichment of material presented. The assignment this week is to examine the assignments you make, their purpose or objective and learner outcome.

1. Log the assignments given in one class each day this week:

a. Assignment _____

   Purpose _____

   Source _____

   Explanation given _____ yes _____ no

   Time appropriate for group _____ yes _____ no

   Completed as planned ____ yes _____ no

   Comment _____

   _____

b. Assignment _____

Purpose _____

Source _____

Explanation given _____ yes _____ no

Time appropriate for group _____ yes _____ no

Completed as planned ____ yes _____ no

Comment _____

_____

c. Assignment _____

Purpose _____

Source _____

Explanation given _____ yes _____ no

Time appropriate for group _____ yes _____ no

Completed as planned ____ yes _____ no

Comment _____

_____

d. Assignment _____

Purpose _____

Source _____

Explanation given _____ yes _____ no

Time appropriate for group _____ yes _____ no

Completed as planned ____ yes _____ no

Comment _____

_____

e. Assignment _____

Purpose _____

Source _____

Explanation given _____ yes _____ no

Time appropriate for group _____ yes _____ no

Completed as planned ____ yes _____ no

Comment _____

_____

2. What techniques are used to handle students neglecting to complete assignments?

_____

_____

_____

_____

_____

_____

Log Excerpts (Making Assignments)

We had a little match before we left. Gave them 17 problems to do. Mrs. A. explained that there will soon be a levels test and they need review. This gives them a purpose--makes work more meaningful.

*****

Both days, I have forgotten to give Michelle and Terrance homework assignments in math. They are on a lower level so they usually can't do the work done by the rest of the class. Mrs. G. did give them assignments though. I need to make sure I have provided for each child in the class. There is so much to think about!

*****

For seat work while one group was at reading, the other group was to write a fable. She discussed fables the other day, played records of some of Aesop's Fables, etc. This seatwork reinforced what a fable was, how to write a paragraph, sentence and story. Plus it provided moral education. Was followed up by some of the kids reading their stories aloud and telling the moral of it. Not all got the idea that a fable has a moral. Needs more work.

*****

I started the day with math. Last week, Ms. C. gave out a graph. Every day, she is assigning a block of the problems either for seatwork or homework. They check their work and then graph how they got correct. Great idea--teaches graphing, motivates, helps student and teacher to see student's progress at a glance.

*****

One of the few advantages of grading English papers is the opportunity to reinforce students personally with comments on papers--I try to do this whenever possible. Many things are revealed by students about themselves in their papers. Much can be gained by scrutinizing their writing carefully--if only it didn't usurp so much time and energy. Already, however, the papers are beginning to improve remarkedly which is somewhat encouraging, even in a sea of discouragement.

*****

Interrupted the "Macbeth" study today in order that the students would have the period to work on a paper (assigned earlier) on Animal Farm. I'm not yet certain whether or not this is a good or bad thing and probably won't know until I recommence the play on Monday.

*****

Ms. B. has seemed to make it clear to children exactly what she expects of them. The assignment directions (for the numbers/colors activity on the board) were to the point and explanatory. She told the children why she gave them that work (to see what numbers and colors they knew) and exactly how she wanted it done.

*****

We have continued to work on my Values learning packet. Students are working hard and seem to be enjoying the activities. They seem to be very motivated to complete the packet. Mrs. H. said today that she is very pleased with the packet. There has been very little I have had to modify. During the period I spend quite a bit of time checking work. This seems to be working also. My directions have needed little extra explaining. It has been interesting to see students working independently. It is obvious that some students are more capable than others. Some are near finishing, others are not so far along.

I worked this past weekend on revising my packet. I have changed nearly all the activities to some extent. Mostly, I have misjudged how long it would take to complete the activities. I also dropped one activity and added another. Some I changed the amount of work that was required. In a few cases I revised the directions.

Further References

Brophy, Jere E. and Carolyn M. Evertson. Learning From Teaching: A Developmental Perspective. Boston: Allyn and Bacon, 1976.

Gage, Nathaniel L. "The Yield of Research on Teaching," Phi Delta Kappan, Vol. 60, No. 3, (November, 1978), 229-235

Good, Thomas L. and Jere E. Brophy. Looking in Classrooms, 3rd ed. New York: Harper and Row Publishers, 1984.

Jarolimek, John and Clifford D. Foster. Teaching and Learning in the Elementary School, 2nd ed. New York: Macmillan Publishing Company, 1981.

Medley, Donald. Teacher Competence and Teaching Effectiveness. Washington, D.C.: AACTE, 1977.

12 Making Assignments

INTERACTION ACTIVITY: **Choice Inscription**

Objectives
To reflect on the choice of a career in teaching.
To identify and publish the self established professional goals.

In the Directory of Occupational Titles, teaching is classified among the service oriented careers. Those choosing to teach are purported to derive job satisfaction from the realization that what they do benefits others dependent on them. Think about the reasons you choose to teach. Look at needs which being a teacher meet and at those needs you expect teaching to satisfy in the future. Consider the degree of verbal, social and nurturing interactions in the school environment. Also think about your interests in ideas and in new learning. Satisfaction in teaching depends on the extent these needs are met through functioning in the teacher role. As you plunge deeper into responsibilities and all other aspects of teaching, you are better able than ever before to compare the benefits you derive from working with students in the school with the expectations you have of a career in teaching.

Becoming immersed in the process of personally learning what becoming a teacher means, while an essential stage, can limit ones view of long range goals. This interaction activity invites you to look ahead and toward the accomplishment stage and at the same time review who and what you intend to be in your chosen career.

Directions and Procedures

Leader: Taking time to reflect on some teacher characteristics is a recurring theme throughout these chapters. In order to give distance from immediate events you are asked to think about inscribing a monument whose message would feature the teacher you aspire to be. This inscription will represent you, the teacher, to those who know you well and to those who never met you nor will ever know you except through reading thoughtfully this inscription. Give the reader as clear an understanding as possible of the characteristics and skills you strive to embody as teacher. These need not be qualities you presently possess.

Extended time with children/youth, with parents, teacher and other supervisors often results in new insights emerging about the importance of knowing, being and doing. This activity invites you to write the abilities you prize and for which you would most be remembered.

Complete the monument inscription as you would like it to read. You will not be asked to display these for others. The message you write is what you would like students to remember about you.

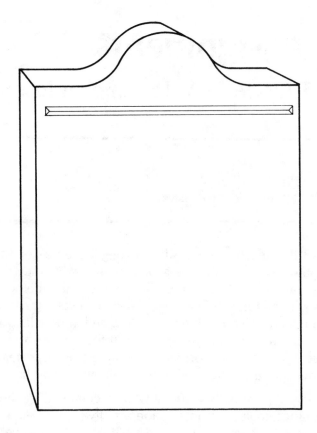

[Allow time to write the inscription. Then, call the group's attention to the process.]

Leader: Each week you are given a reflection topic emphasizing one or more attitudes or personal qualities. Then, there is the group process which is intended to help you acquire greater self knowledge and increase self acceptance. These different parts of the interaction activities can be incorporated into thoughts and actions towards yourself and others and can affect your manner of behaving. New behavior becomes part of you with frequent repetition. Examine the list of characteristics by which you want to be remembered. Is there one listed which is new or for which you described a new dimension? Why have you listed what you did? Turn to another person in the group and explain some "new" part of the listing and explain why.

[After 5-8 minutes call the total group's attention to the Discussion Questions or close the activity with comments applying the topic to specific school situations.]

Discussion Questions

Leader: A. To what extent are expectations you have of a career in teaching similar to earlier ideas you remember?
B. Did the "inscribe a monument" task draw your attention toward the future, the past or where? Explain.
C. When would you suggest repeating this activity for yourself and other teachers you know?
D. How might you use this activity with your students?

SKILL ACTIVITY: **Assignments**

Objectives
To examine oral and written assignments for learner outcome.
To develop, use and evaluate appropriate instructional activities for individual or group assignments.

Assignment of instructional activities and material can provide reinforcement, enrichment and challenge to the learner. Knowing when to schedule assignments, the amount of time required to complete each activity and the learning outcome for the individuals involved is essential to good planning. During this week you have examined assignments given to learners. Your insights to the following questions will contribute to discussion.

1. Select one activity you assigned this week. Share the purpose for the assignment. To what exent was the intended learner outcome achieved?
2. How are assignments ususally determined for each class?
3. Are individual differences taken into consideration when assignments are made?
4. To what extent are directions and explanations clearly stated for all assignments?
5. Is there independent working after assignment has been given the learner?
6. What types of written and oral assignments were used in your class/es during the week? Comment on their effectiveness for learners involved in the activities.
7. Were all assignments completed by every student? How were students who "forgot" or failed to complete assignments handled?

Assignment (Evaluating Learner Performance)

Assessment is essential for improvement of the curriculum of teaching and for student learning. It is imperative that the assessment procedures used in the classroom reflect the instructional objectives of the teacher if they are to influence and impact the learning process designed to achieve these objectives. Properly designed assessment instruments and procedures can improve decision making regarding learner performance. In addition, the instructional strategies implemented in the educational experience must be geared to the achievement of the stated objectives. You will examine assessment instruments and their use in gathering evaluative evidence of learner achievement.

1. Select one or two learners from your class. Study their academic achievement records as indicated by test scores. Compare their day-to-day performance with the cumulative record.

Student #1 _____ Grade Level _____ Age

Test Scores	Math	Reading	____	_____
198 ___	_____	_____	_____	_____
198 ___	_____	_____	_____	_____
198 ___	_____	_____	_____	_____

Comments on test scores _____

_____

Comparison: record and daily performance _____

_____

_____

_____

_____

_____

Student #2 _____ Grade Level _____ Age

Test Scores	Math	Reading	____	____
198 ____	____	____	____	____
198 ____	____	____	____	____
198 ____	____	____	____	____

Comments on test scores _____

_____

Comparison: record and daily performance _____

_____

_____

_____

_____

2. Examine a set of tests or assignments given students. Analyze the learner responses and the distribution of grades. Did you meet the instructional objectives planned? How do you inform the students who need remediation? Comment:

_____

_____

_____

_____

_____

_____

_____

_____

_____

_____

_____

_____

_____

_____

_____

_____

_____

_____

_____

3. Which of the following assessment instruments have you examined and/or used with learners?

Assessment Devices	Examined	Used
Observation		
Group discussion		
Interview		
Checklists		
Inventories		
Questionnaires		
Logs		
Autobiographies		
Collections		
Samples of work		
Teacher made tests		
Standardized tests		
Cumulative records		
Tape recordings		
Case studies		
Sociograms		

Log Excerpts (Evaluating Learner Performance)

This morning Ms. C. and I previewed some of the math levels tests. I am going to give the levels test to my own group before I leave. We both feel that this will be a good experience for me.

*****

. . . I worked with two students on one of their seatwork activities--clocks. They have had a hard time putting the numbers in the correct places on the clockfaces. I drew faces and drilled them on the positions of the numbers, the length of the hands and where to have the hands pointed for specific times. Their papers look magnificently better! And they did it themselves.

*****

Miss B. tested Clair with informal reading inventory the first week of school because her report card from the last school was so vague and inconsistent. Clair did not do at all well on the IRI. In the reading group she doesn't know a lot of the words and frequently has to ask for help. On the other hand, however, she seems to be comprehending a great deal of what she reads. She always has her hand raised to answer questions about the passage.

*****

I've decided to observe a student in one of my freshman classes because Mr. D. has been told that he is having some problems adjusting. Mr. D. already has tried to get him involved in the yearbook photography group.

*****

I did make the effort today to call on this student--even though his hand wasn't up (funny, I felt I could almost feel, in his eyes, a desire to be called on.) As I suspected, he had a pretty good answer ready which I was happy to hear. Unfortunately, I didn't seize the opportunity to reinfore him like I should have.

*****

I think my observation of this particular student has helped me more in my observation of all my students than I had previously imagined. When one realizes that one particular student is much more than a face and a set of responses, one must also realize that all students are much more than we ever get to see on the surface.

*****

I compared the tests I scored yesterday, to see areas that need to be retaught. Have some trouble with antonyms, possessives, time element and capitalization/punctuation. A lot of the problem, I think, is the directions on the test. Either what they were to look for was unclear or the method of responding was difficult to understand. The big problems were with probable outcome, topic sentences and fact/opinion. These are areas we have not spent much time on and it shows.

*****

All day, I checked the language arts levels test. I found it really interesting to see the scores. Tomorrow, I am going to take a closer look at them--compare to see who needs remediation, if scores support the way we have the students divided into two groups, plus where teaching weaknesses are. I can already tell some inconsistencies in our grouping--we had some doubts about the groups a few kids were in. This test confirms our suspicions that they could do better in the other group.

*****

Tomorrow progress reports are distributed. The grades are cumulative for the past twelve weeks. This is somewhat unfortunate for these students who did nothing the first six weeks. There are some students who have no chance of passing for this semester. They have no chance of passing, even if they score perfectly these next six weeks. Our procedure for giving grades is a simple one. Yesterday we figured grades, today we told students individually what their grades were, tomorrow we will fill in their progress reports. Our intent was to avoid grade discussions tomorrow while we are busy filling out the progress reports. The reports ask for a lot of information. If we spent time arguing and explaining grades, we would not have enough time to complete all the reports.

Most of our students are passing. A few have no chance of passing and will fail. We are beginning to individualize lessons more and more. Giving failing grades is not pleasureable. Helping students achieve is much more worthwhile.

Further References

Ahmann, J.S. and M.D. Glock. <u>Evaluating Student Progress: Principles of Tests and Measurements</u>, 6th ed. Boston: Allyn and Bacon, 1981.

Ebel, Robert L. <u>Essentials of Educational Measurement</u>, 2nd ed. Englewood Cliffs, New Jersey: Prentice-Hall, 1979.

Gagne, Robert M. and Leslie J. Briggs. <u>Principles of Instructional Design</u>, 2nd ed. New York: Holt, Rinehart and Winston, 1979.

Gronlund, Norman E. <u>Constructing Achievement Tests.</u> Englewood Cliffs, New Jersey: Prentice-Hall, 1977.

Hannah, Larry S. and John U. Michaelis. <u>A Comprehensive Framework for Instructional Objectives: A Guide to Systematic Planning and Evaluation.</u> Reading, Massachusetts: Addison Wesley Publishing Company, 1977.

Jacobsen, David, Paul Eggen, Donald Kauchak, et. al. <u>Methods for Teaching: A Skills Approach</u>, 2nd ed. Columbus, Ohio: Charles E. Merrill Publishing Company, 1985.

Popham, W. James. <u>Criterion Referenced Measurement.</u> Englewood Cliffs, New Jersey: Prentice-Hall, 1978.

Ten Brink, Terry D. <u>Evaluation: A Practical Guide for Teachers.</u> New York: McGraw-Hill Book Company, 1974.

13 Evaluating Learner Performance
INTERACTION ACTIVITY: Acknowledging Assets

Objectives
To recognize ways that teachers can influence learners.
To examine occurring changes in ones own perceptions in becoming a teacher.

Teachers foster student attitudes. This means that teacher beliefs and behaviors when deliberately communicated, heighten student awareness of attitudes encouraged by the school and society in general. These include attitudes toward self and others and the acknowledgement that much which appears ordinary, is available to us through the ideals and efforts of others. Teachers, appreciative of who they are and of the benefits they have received, can be expected to draw student attention to routine events and to take special notice of school community, state and national celebrations. Whether it be a simple verbal reminder or a complicated project, the teacher's internalization of the event can be significant to student response.

Directions and Procedures

[The Leader establishes a setting appropriate to the group process.]

Leader: Other Interaction Activities have directed you to reflect on gifts and abilities you possess. This one looks beyond your own person to gifts reflected in ideals such as freedom, love of country, dignity of work, fidelity to family and friends. As a beginning teacher you may become aware of personal strengths you previously took for granted. Amidst the United States' plenty there are children and youth needing nurturing if not nourishment. You may have contrasted the difference in your life style and life goals with that of your students. At least one time a year TV commercials and other advertisements repeatedly expose the public to themes acknowledging and giving thanks for the bounty enjoyed in our country. Cornucopia, Pilgrims, turkeys and other displayed symbols call our attention to the ideal being celebrated. Think of the many bulletin boards throughout the school. In what way does this celebration time have a different meaning to you as you begin teaching? Pause for a few minutes allowing yourself to examine the personal strengths you have come to prize during this past year. Which gifts have enabled you to teach?

[Allow 3-4 minutes for quiet reflection time. Emphasize and encourage students to name a single personal strength on which they rely as teacher.]

Leader: Each week we have you form a group and ask you to consciously separate your thoughts from the classroom, the school and the rush-about-pace. Within this familiar space and with these people you are asked to quietly be present to yourself. Becoming a reflective teacher requires that you begin now to allow yourself to pause and look at what you are doing, being and becoming. Without reflection self evaluation has little depth and less impact on subsequent performance.

As a group member you can contribute and gain from others perceptions. All are encourged to express insights and to respond to questions asked. For some, talking about feelings and insights may seem risky. It will not be easy; growth seldom is. Sharing with one other person is less scary than describing yourself to an entire group. Again today we ask you to look for someone with whom you have not shared.

Tell the person about some strength or value of which you now claim but would have taken for granted a year ago. When you are the receiver, pay special attention to the speaker. Let that person know s/he is being heard.

[After 5-8 minutes call the total group's attention to the following questions.]

Discussion Questions

Leader: A. Did anyone recall past teachers who made you aware of your abilities? Friends? Parents?
B. How many named freedom, love of family and friends or other benefits you would want your students to recall?
C. To what extent are expressions of gratitude more important to you now as you move closer to becoming teacher? Can you say why this may happen?

SKILL ACTIVITY: **Evaluating Learner Performance**

Objectives

To examine cumulative records for making classroom evaluations.
To develop test items for assessing learner achievement.
To examine and use appropriate assessment instruments for obtaining evaluative information about learner and learner performance.

Learner performance is evaluated to determine the extent to which objectives have been achieved and to make better decisions in planning curriculum and instruction. Research has found that effective teachers collect, organize and interpret evaluative evidence of learner progress and make changes to improve instruction. Using the following questions, share the results you found from examining and using assessment instruments.

1. From whom did you obtain cumulative records? In your comparison of the learner's daily performance with the cumulative record data, what similarities and/or differences were evident?
2. How is this information valuable for instructional planning?
3. To what extent do your teacher-made test items correspond with the objectives stated in lesson plans for the particular content area?
4. How was grading determined? Were any provisions made for exceptional learners?
5. Share with the group some insights gained from the test results. Will you make changes in your curriculum plans or instructional strategies from the evaluative results?
6. Which assessment instruments did you find useful in obtaining information about learner performance?

*****

Assignment (Remediation and Reinforcement)

Assessment information assists the teacher in development of instructional techniques and materials suitable for varied learner capabilities. You have examined and analyzed evaluative instruments and information regarding learner performance. Within the classroom you find a number of exceptional students whose achievement may be far above grade level and present a challenging experience preparing materials for them. Other learners may require a special remedial program or plan. And some learners' progress depends on repetition, drill and other reinforcement techniques. The following activities present an opportunity to focus on various types of materials, plans and techniques used in accommodating for all learners.

1. To accommodate varied learning abilities, how many of the following procedures are used with your class or group:

Used	Procedure	Subject	# of students
	Individual Education Plan (IEP)		
	Grouping (Reading, Math)		
	Learning Centers/Packets		
	Independent Work		
	Contracts		
	Group Discussion		
	Projects		
	Written Reinforcement Activities (activity/ practice sheets, skill booklets, composition)		

2. Select concepts taught in classes this week.
   ex. least common multiple, agreement of pronoun with verbs.

   Complete the following for each concept:

Concept _____

    Presented/explained (tally) _____

    Reinforced (tally no. of times) _____

    Assessment (name procedure) _____

    _____

    Remediation (list plan) _____

    _____

    _____

Concept _____

    Presented/explained (tally) _____

    Reinforced (tally no. of times) _____

Assessment (name procedure) _____

_____

Remediation (list plan) _____

_____

_____

Concept _____

Presented/explained (tally) _____

Reinforced (tally no. of times) _____

Assessment (name procedure) _____

_____

Remediation (list plan) _____

_____

_____

Concept _____

Presented/explained (tally) _____

Reinforced (tally no. of times) _____

Assessment (name procedure) _____

_____

Remediation (list plan) _____

_____

_____

Log Excerpts (Remediating and Accommodating Learner Performance)

I just finished working with a small group on subtracting and borrowing. They are really beginning to catch on. All next week I am going to drill this group on borrowing, working for measurable success by Thursday. If not, we will continue.

*****

I handled the discussion this morning after third period. I was surprised at the good responses to questions given by third period. One student in particular who usually does not participate in discussions gave an excellent thought-through answer. It was a good achievement for her and I hope I gave her the necessary and proper reinforcement.

*****

Also tried to re-emphasize my O Twist points today when discussing the dramatic presentations. This was also effective, I felt, but it does have limitations in literature. There is still, that whole aesthetic side to literature which cannot be passed on through drilling and through study. The teacher must spill a little blood for this transformation to occur. I think the attitude and actions of the teacher influence students in this area more than anything the teacher says.

*****

I checked math levels test that they took Wednesday. Did great--most mistakes were simple addition, subtraction, multiplication mistakes. Everyone passed--only about three people made below the criterion on a subtest. She discussed the scores as a whole, went over some problem areas, told a few individuals their problem areas (embarrassed some of them--should have done it in private). Kids are happy with their scores overall.

*****

I am beginning to see the importance of review and reiteration in teaching. It seems to me that if a teacher can narrow down a lesson to several important points which s/he is going to emphasize and reemphasize, that teacher has done much to present the lesson in a way that the student knows which steps he/she must take in order to comprehend, remember, and use the information in a meaningful way.

*****

Kids this age, I have noticed, still have trouble in most games working as a team, keeping their position, etc.

*****

Today in reading (Steelers) I used a checklist. I told them I was checking names of those who gave good answers and would base my grade on it. Helped to motivate. Also I have a record of who answers and who didn't. I'll keep this up and look for patterns. Also helped me make sure I gave everyone a chance.

*****

It is good to know that the kids who aren't such top readers can sometimes excell the top kids in math or other subjects. This is happening frequently in the math drill at the board.

*****

Ms. C. is teaching one of the Phonics groups now. Her questioning includes recognition of short vowel sounds and asking them to supply words with short vowel sounds. She continually asks for them to repeat directions that she has given them in order to give them the opportunity to reinforce what is to be done. Ms. C. gives a lot of verbal reinforcement when it is earned.

*****

Ms. S. is now drilling the kids on the day, month, season, etc. She is also helping them understand that yesterday was Wednesday, tomorrow is Friday, last month was September. The word of the day is emergency. She first had the students attempt to read it. Then they talked about the meaning of emergency, how they would feel during an emergency, and what they should do during an emergency.

Further References

Alschuler, Alfred S. Development Achievement Motivation in Adolescents. Englewood Cliffs, New Jersey: Educational Technology Publications, 1973.

Bee, Clifford P. Secondary Learners Centers. Santa Monica: Goodyear Publishing Company, 1980.

Clark, Leonard H. and Irving S. Starr. Secondary and Middle School Teaching Methods, 4th ed. New York: Macmillan Publishing Company, 1981.

Gage, Nathaniel L. "The Yield of Research on Teaching", Phi Delta Kappan. Vol. 60, No. 3, (November, 1978), 229-235.

Gagne, Robert M. and Leslie J. Briggs. Principles of Instructional Design, 2nd ed. New York: Holt, Rinehart and Winston, 1979.

Good, Thomas L. and Jere E. Brophy. Looking in Classrooms, 3rd ed. New York: Harper and Row, 1984.

Henson, Kenneth T. Secondary Teaching Methods. Lexington, Massachusetts: D.C. Heath and Company, 1981.

Jersild, Arthur T. When Teachers Face Themselves. New York: Teachers College Press, Columbia University, 1955.

Mercer, Cecil D. and Ann R. Mercer. Teaching Students with Learning Problems. Columbus, Ohio: Charles E. Merrill Publishing Company, 1981.

Ward, Patricia S. And E. Craig Williams. Learning Packets. West Nyack: Parker Publishing Company, 1976.

Whitmore, Joanne Rand. Giftedness, Conflict and Underachievement. Boston: Allyn and Bacon, 1980.

14 Remediating and Accommodating Learner Performance

INTERACTION ACTIVITY: Questioning the Question

Objectives

To reflect on the process of becoming TEACHER.
To state one question which characterizes your concerns at this time.

Beginning to teach is a period of intense professional and personal growth, a time of becoming. In addition to applying skills and knowledge from earlier campus courses to specific learners over an extended time period, you are adjusting to the demanding pace of teaching. For some, this initial assumption of responsibility for a group is psychologically, physically and emotionally draining. On the other hand, you are introspective about your progress as teacher and continually assess your ability to communicate and at the same time you are selecting and preparing strategies and materials intended to meet learner needs.

Taking time to reflect on this BECOMING process is important for growth and learning. Of its nature reflection is a product of self choosing. While being a group member encourages involvement in the reflective process presented through these Interaction Activities, the degree of self understanding and acceptance attained depends on each participant's response. The BECOMING process will not always be comfortable; some may experience disappointment and pain. Nonetheless, the importance of this process extends throughout the teaching career. Teachers who understand and accept themselves are better able to help students know themselves and to gain healthy attitudes of self acceptance.

Directions and Procedures

[Frequently and clearly communicating the purpose of the group process for beginning teachers is an essential leader function if participants are to integrate the interaction and skill activities into their own teacher behaviors.]

Leader: You are nearing the final weeks as a beginning teacher. Now, as in former weeks, you are asked to think about some aspect of yourself as teacher. There are four stages which seem to describe persons at various intervals in their initial teaching experiences.

First: Concern about self. Where do I stand in this situation and what do people (superiors and administrators) want from me?

Second: Concern about ones adequacy in the teaching role. Do I know what I am teaching? Will I know what to say? Will I say it correctly?

Third: Concern about discipline. Students continue talking while I talk or other students are giving their response. How can I get my class to attend to the tasks given?

Fourth: Concern about what your students are learning. Who can work a problem? What is another way I can review this topic or concept? Should I spend more time on this material or continue and reteach it at a later date?

Reviewing these stages do you recall a time during the past week when you asked yourself one of the questions stated above? You may have caught yourself mulling over one student wondering what to do. What was your concern for that student? Take some time to consider questions you may or may not have shared with others. Focus on a single concern and examine what questions you were asking?

[Encourage participants to select a single question they recall having about one student or several. Allow 2-4 minutes of quiet before continuing with the following.]

Leader: One of the learnings which usually comes from the group process is that others have similar thoughts and questions. After you seek out some person with whom you have not shared before, take turns telling the other about a question you have asked yourself during the past week. Make certain the other understands your question. One way the listener can do this is by rephrasing the message heard.

[Allow 6-8 minutes and then call together the total group.]

Discussion Questions

Leader: Being willing to share your questions with one person can be somewhat difficult and sharing with a large group is generally a little risky. You have taken risks before in this group and in your classroom. Little growth is possible without some risk. In this situation there are common feelings and awarenesses due to the fact that all are at the beginning stage of a career. You were asked to reflect on questions of concern about students. Would you comment on:

A. What are some of the questions being asked?

B. In what ways has this reflection included an awareness of changes in your perceptions during the past months?

C. Which other interaction activity caused you to face new information about your "self?"

D. Name one self awareness which you want to recall often.

SKILL ACTIVITY: **Remediation and Reinforcement**

Objectives
To plan and provide instruction accommodating for differences in learner ability and learning rates using assessment results.

To provide frequent and varied practice of skills.

To reassess learner progress and revise objectives accordingly.

Providing instruction for varying learner abilities requires special skill. Effective teachers involve the whole class, encourage response from all learners and provide immediate feedback to the learner. Recognition of the need for reinforcement and remediation together with developing materials and techniques for teaching to varied learner abilities is no small task for the beginning teacher. You have identified learning problems and planned or refined instructional materials for remediation.. Furthermore, you have directed attention to and practiced reinforcement techniques in lesson presentations. Share some of these experiences using the following activities:

1. Select a procedure from the chart you used in accommodating for varied learning abilities in your class or group.
   a. Describe the procedure and tell to what extent it enabled learners to meet the intended instructional objectives. (Was the procedure intended for a specific group? Were other procedures or techniques just as appropriate for this class of learners? Which ones?)
   b. What problems were encountered in planning instruction to suit learner abilities? (Were materials readily available? Units, learning center/packets, individualized activities and other teacher made materials may be introduced and/or used at this time?)
2. Choose one particular concept taught this week:
   a. Describe the presentation, reinforcement and assessment of the concept. (Were remediation steps part of the process if learners had difficulty grasping the content?)
   b. To what extent were steps taken to ensure learner achievement? (Were the teacher expectations too high? Was time a factor?)

*****

Assignment (Reporting to Parents)

Traditionally, the report card has been the principle link in the communication process between the school and the parent or guardian. More recently, emphasis has been placed on increased parental involvement within the schools. Parent-teacher conferences and school meetings have been met with more support and cooperation from parents or guardians and teachers.

Responsibility for completing report cards or preparing conference reports for parents or guardians may not be entirely your task at this time. Assisting the supervising or another teacher develop the total report by sharing the grades and evaluative information you have recorded will add to your confidence and competence as teacher. The activities below draw attention to the various aspects of the learner evaluation report to parents and guardians undertaken by the school and teacher.

1. Bring to the seminar a blank report card or progress form used in your school.

2. Discuss with your supervising or another teacher the plans used by the school and teachers for reporting to parents or guardians.
   Open House _____

   _____

   _____

   _____

   _____

   Parent Teacher Conferences _____

   _____

   _____

   _____

   Report Cards/Progress Reports _____

   _____

   _____

   _____

   IEP _____

   _____

   _____

   _____

   Parent Teacher Organization Meetings _____

   _____

   _____

   _____

3. Please tally the number of times these periodic and systematic evaluative reports were given students during this week:

Reports	Mon.	Tues.	Wed.	Thurs.	Fri.
1. Tests					
2. Daily Assignments					
3. Projects					
4. Class Participation					
5. Notebook/Lab Books					
6. Home/Assignments					
7. Other					

Log Excerpts (Reporting to Parents)

Looked at student with somewhat of a different eye today. Yesterday was a day when parents were invited to come and meet their child's teacher . . .

In checking over the list of parents who did come, it appeared that about half of the students' parents came. Yesterday it seemed like we talked to about 5,000 parents. Apparently to have a satisfactory conference one must set aside a good block of time. (Many of our talks were very quick owing the long line of parents waiting to get in.) I was a little surprised how long it takes to see forty to fifty parents.

*****

Report cards go home tomorrow. I looked over them. Mrs. A. graded them according to how they were doing based on their own ability--not in relation to the rest of the class. Good--it wouldn't be fair or true if for instance Terrance who is on level 9 is compared to Dana on level 14. There are many A's and B's. It is no bell curve. Yet, I think they earned them; the kids work hard. Those who don't do as well as they could, got C's. I can't see assigning lower grades just to meet a theoretical curve. The card had a list of things that if checked meant the kid needed improvement in that area.

*****

I sat in on the conference with Mrs. O. the other day. She seems to be really willing to work with Andy. We were previously concerned that she was giving in to Andy and babying him too much. But she is, if anything, tougher than we are on him. She also mentioned to Ms. S. the possibility of him being emotionally disturbed. I have no idea if his problem can be classified so seriously but I do think that it is big of her to at least admit the possibility.

*****

I really do wish kids would not be so protected by their parents, sometimes. The sun really will come up tomorrow, compositions notwithstanding! Such behavior seems terribly self-centered and growth prohibitive. It is hard to release kids on the road to maturity when parents will not support. Such behavior results in really negative behavior from the child--EVERYTHING becomes a chore when such shielding is imposed. How is the kid ever gonna learn how to enjoy?

*****

Miss B. is sending a letter to parents, telling them that the students have been working on the time concept and that they need to practice it at home every night. I love the way she "invites" the parents to accept responsibility for helping their children learn. It is certainly something they need to be doing.

*****

It is interesting to note how teachers deal with phone calls from parents. It is encouraging to see parents call when their child is having trouble. Often, the phone calls are nothing more than information gathering sessions; rarely do parents suspect teachers before they suspect their children. And, usually, the student's work/behavior improves remarkedly after such a phone call. There have been one or two instances where parents have been irate, but not nearly so often as I had previously expected. When they are, it is often frustrating because I find the irate (from my observation--no actual experience) ones are philosophically simply on different planes than I think I would be. It is difficult to communicate when either side isn't hearing/doesn't want to listen to the other.

*****

Today grades were distributed. It's interesting how some students are interested in grades only six times a year. The two times the semester ends and the four times progress reports are distributed are peak interest times. There are some students who promise the moon to improve. They sell their soul trying to convince you that they will improve. As a teacher, I feel and see how important the beginning of the year is. As I begin school years in the future, I plan on spending some valuable time explaining just how grades are figured. I feel it is important for students to know where they stand at the beginning. I know much of this work at the beginning will be falling on deaf ears. This will require the time of explaining and reevaluating progress a short time after the year has begun.

Further References

Berger, Eugenia Hepworth. Parents as Partner in Education. St. Louis: The C.V. Mosby Company, 1981

Brandt, Ronald, ed. Partners: Parents and Schools. Alexandria, Virginia: ASCD, 1979.

Fantini, Mario D. What's Best for the Children: Resolving the Power Struggle Between Parents and Teachers. Garden City: New York: Anchor Books, 1975.

Gordon, K.J. and W.F. Breivogel, eds. Building Effective Home/School Relationships. Boston: Allyn and Bacon, 1976.

Kroth, Roger L. and Richard L. Simpson. Parent Conferences as a Teaching Strategy. Denver: Love Publishing Company, 1977.

Rutherford, Robert B., Jr. and Eugene Edgar. Teachers and Parents: A Guide to Interaction and Cooperation, abridged ed. Boston: Allyn and Bacon, 1979.

15 Reporting to Parents
INTERACTION ACTIVITY: Reflective Reviewing

Objective
To recall personal learning from progress reporting and to reflect on the desirable knowledge and attitude needed by teachers.

Indirectly related to reporting to parents is the teacher's ability to specify the results of striving for established goals. This includes not only such goals as clear communication with others but also the ability to perceive and articulate the long and short-range learner outcomes. The best review is accomplished from acquiring an overview of the total skill or concept being studied and a recognition of each separate part. What you learn from assessing and stating your own progress and relying on specific evidence for doing so, applies to progress reporting with parents and learners.

A blending of strengths and limitations, encourages a sense of balance in the reporting process. You may need to emphasize this balance to both learners and parents. Again, your own learning can help prepare you for these situations. Many agree that assessment by self and/or others which emphasizes an ability or accomplishment releases ego strength which in turn can be focused toward recognizing and accepting areas of weakness. Employ a sense of time and perspective as you reflect on what was helpful to you as learner. Decide how you might communicate this to those with few specific goals and to those whose accomplishments scarcely match their stated goals.

Directions and Procedures

[The Leader establishes the tone for the group activity.]

Leader: Practicing skills and integrating theory have been continuous throughout the past months. One area requiring skill, knowledge and attitude is progress reporting. Think about what evidence you accumulated to show student and/or parents progress made and areas for improvement. Why did you select the particular evidence? What attitude did you intend to communicate? To what extent did your own learning influence the means used to communicate the progress or need-for-progress message to parents/students?

[Allow 2-4 minutes for participants to reflect upon one or more points emphasized.]

Leader: Using your own or a supervisor's experience with reporting progress to students and parents describe to another group member the learning you have gained. Explain in what way the process was new for you. Include anything you learned which you intend to practice in future interactions of this kind.

[Allow 5-6 minutes and then call together the total group.]

Discussion Questions

Leader: Parents and teacher are partners in the education of children and youth. Although you may have limited opportunity to talk with parents, you have conferenced with students about grades.
  A. What attitudes would you prefer having when reporting progress to parents? To students?
  B. In what way might your experiences with assessment prepare you for conferencing with parents?
  C. What fear might beginning teachers have about reporting to parents? students?

SKILL ACTIVITY: **Reporting to Parents**

Objectives
To organize evaluative information for reporting to parents or guardians.
To communicate learner needs and achievements to parents and learner.
To obtain important information from parents and teachers to assist in planning appropriate curriculum for all learners.

Current research suggests a partner relationship between parent and teacher results in better learning for students. Reporting to parents or guardians can be an effective means of creating and continuing cooperative relationships between home and school. In addition, communication between parent, guardian and teacher can serve as encouragement and direction for the learner if appropriate information is shared. You have discovered through discussions with the supervising or cooperative teacher how essential it is to be well prepared and organized when reporting to parents or guardians. Response to the following questions can be shared with others:

1. What do parents want to know about school in relationship to their son or daughter? How important is it that you know the skills taught, learner capabilities, homework assignments, learner social behaviors, learner's performance on tests, schedule of learner activities, classroom management strategies, etc.?
2. What information does the teacher want from parents regarding the learner?
3. How does the teacher communicate to the learner the grades recorded on the progress report?
4. Using the evaluative information from the assignment, what value do you place on each type of report?

*****

Assignment (Assessing the Role of Teacher)

Assuming the total responsibility for planning and instruction of learners requires commitment and stamina. Teaching can be an exciting, rewarding and sometimes awesome experience. Unless skilled in self evaluation, you may be limited to emotional feeling regarding your response to instruction. (ex. "I felt good about my match lesson today", or "It was fun experience for my students.") Throughout the beginning teaching experience you have been assigned activities to increase your confidence and competence in the teaching role. You have become a perceptive observer and initiated participation in all teaching tasks. Furthermore, you have planned, prepared and actually taught learners with varied abilities. This assignment requires examining an entire class instruction from preparation through assessment, thus focusing on your instructional behaviors.

1. Log the assessment of your instruction of one class each day this week. Include the following components:

Class _____ Subject _____

Preparation for the class _____

_____

_____

_____

Effecting the learning atmosphere _____

_____

_____

_____

_____

_____

Presentation

Introduction: _____

_____

_____

_____

Stimulus Variation: _____

_____

_____

_____

Closure or Review: _____

_____

_____

_____

Methods used: _____ direct instruction, _____ inquiry,

_____ group investigation, _____ discussion, _____ learning centers/packets,

_____ creative problem solving.

Materials used: _____ text, _____ concrete objects _____ film strips,

_____ overhead projector, _____ chalkboard, _____ maps, _____ chart,

_____ graphics, _____ supplementary activities.

Performance of the learners: _____

_____

_____

_____

Assessment instruments used: _____

_____

_____

_____

Class _____ Subject _____

Preparation for the class _____

_____

_____

_____

Effecting the learning atmosphere _____

_____

_____

_____

Presentation

    Introduction: _____

_____

_____

_____

    Stimulus Variation: _____

_____

_____

_____

    Closure or Review: _____

_____

_____

_____

Methods used: _____ direct instruction, _____ inquiry, _____ group investigation, _____ discussion, _____ learning centers/packets, _____ creative problem solving.

Materials used: _____ text, _____ concrete objects _____ film strips, _____ overhead projector, _____ chalkboard, _____ maps, _____ chart, _____ graphics, _____ supplementary activities.

Performance of the learners: _____

_____

_____

_____

Assessment instruments used: _____

_____

_____

_____

Class _____ Subject _____

Preparation for the class _____

_____

_____

_____

Effecting the learning atmosphere _____

_____

_____

_____

Presentation

    Introduction: _____

_____

_____

_____

    Stimulus Variation: _____

_____

_____

_____

    Closure or Review: _____

_____

_____

_____

Methods used: _____ direct instruction, _____ inquiry,
_____ group investigation, _____ discussion, _____ learning centers/packets,
_____ creative problem solving.

Materials used: _____ text, _____ concrete objects _____ film strips,
_____ overhead projector, _____ chalkboard, _____ maps, _____ chart,
_____ graphics, _____ supplementary activities.

Performance of the learners: _____

_____

_____

_____

Assessment instruments used: _____

_____

_____

_____

Class _____ Subject _____

Preparation for the class _____

_____

_____

Effecting the learning atmosphere _____

_____

_____

_____

Presentation

Introduction: _____

_____

_____

_____

Stimulus Variation: _____

_____

_____

_____

Closure or Review: _____

_____

_____

_____

Methods used: _____ direct instruction, _____ inquiry,

_____ group investigation, _____ discussion, _____ learning centers/packets,

_____ creative problem solving.

Materials used: _____ text, _____ concrete objects _____ film strips,

_____ overhead projector, _____ chalkboard, _____ maps, _____ chart,

_____ graphics, _____ supplementary activities.

Performance of the learners: _____

_____

_____

_____

Assessment instruments used: _____

_____

_____

_____

Class _____ Subject _____

Preparation for the class _____

_____

_____

_____

Effecting the learning atmosphere _____

_____

_____

_____

Presentation

  Introduction: _____
_____
_____
_____

  Stimulus Variation: _____
_____
_____
_____

  Closure or Review: _____
_____
_____
_____

Methods used: _____ direct instruction, _____ inquiry,
_____ group investigation, _____ discussion, _____ learning centers/packets,
_____ creative problem solving.
Materials used: _____ text, _____ concrete objects _____ film strips,
_____ overhead projector, _____ chalkboard, _____ maps, _____ chart,
_____ graphics, _____ supplementary activities.
Performance of the learners: _____
_____
_____
_____

Assessment instruments used: _____
_____
_____
_____

Log Excerpts (Assessing Teaching Performance)

Sixth period civics is an interesting class. Today we finished a reading activity that we've been working on for a few days. We read short sections in the book and look for the main idea. The intent is to show the students how main ideas can be found. As long as control is gained from the onset, effective learning atmospheres can be had. Today was no exception. There are enough students in this class capable of advanced work that they realize when to be quiet. Preparing for classes has been easy this week. I have worked hard this semester on varying the lesson. My students do not work for more than twenty-five minutes on any one activity. Today was no exception. I see the essential importance of providing choice and reinforcement. It is an attention-grabber. It's not as effective as an overhead but still useful to focus attention. Students performed well today. The notes that they took were complete and done carefully. It was a successful lesson.

*****

As I get more and more familiar with teaching science, it becomes easier. I had to prepare for the lesson by getting the materials I needed together . . . sugar and salt solution and gingerbread. The students responded enthusiastically to the idea of smelling and tasting, etc. The stimulus variation involved the various experiments, the discussion of vocabulary and diagrams and the telecast which was a reinforcement of my lesson. The closure consisted of a short review and suggestions for further experiments at home. The students behaved in a very mature manner. The more we do experiments like this, the more I realize what behavior is expected of them and it becomes natural for them. The evaluation was the oral discussion, the work in their notebook and their participation in the experiment.

*****

Well, Thanksgiving has come and gone---whether or not I've "got it by Thanksgiving" is not entirely clear to me at this point. There are things I do know--e.g. certain student's specific problems, which students I need to call on more in class, which parts of my presentation I need to focus on most, some techniques which have been particularly effective for me, etc. However, there are things I wish I had a better grasp of--e.g. when do I know that a student(s) has not really grasped a concept even though he/she is making motions indicating that he/she has? How can I pick up a "dead" class on Monday morning? How can I better make students want to read? When exactly do I get honest with students and say "No!" and when do I ease up and still try to remain positive? All are things which are going to take a lot more time and experience. Nevertheless, I do feel quite capable of teaching now. I even look forward to trying to do what I can to fulfill the vision of education I see and that vision as I fit into it.

*****

Ms. C. and I talked today about her leaving the room. She says she feels confident that I am honest with her about what goes on when she's gone. Of course I am!

*****

I had a day that Ms. B. calls "normal". I had interruptions, scheduling changes and an assembly. She was out of the room for most of the day. I talked with her this afternoon about how I handled it all. She reinforced me and approved.

Further References

Bloom, Benjamin. All Our Children Learning. St. Louis: McGraw-Hill Book Company, 1981.

Good, Thomas L. and Jere E. Brophy. Looking In Classrooms, 3rd ed. New York: Harper and Row, 1984.

Hoover, Kenneth H. The Professional Teacher's Handbook. Boston: Allyn and Bacon, 1982.

Howey, Kenneth R. and William E. Gardner. The Education of Teachers: A Look Ahead. New York: Longman, 1983.

Jacobsen, David, et. al. Methods for Teaching: A Skills Approach, 2nd ed. Columbus, Ohio: Charles E. Merrill Publishing Company, 1985.

Lewis, James J. Appraising Teacher Performance. West Nyack, New York: Parker Publishing Company, 1973.

Medley, Donald L., et. al. Measurement-Based Evaluation of Teacher Performance. New York: Longman, 1984.

Orlich, Donald C., et. al. Teaching Strategies, 2nd ed. Lexington, Massachusetts: D.C. Heath and Company, 1985.

Roe, Betty D., et. al. Student Teaching And Field Experiences Handbook. Columbus, Ohio: Charles E. Merrill Publishing Company, 1984.

16 Assessing Teaching Performance
INTERACTION ACTIVITY: **Professionally Yours**

Objective
To consider and list demonstrated abilities and areas needing further strengthening.

This final chapter specifically centers on participant ability to self evaluate and to recognize the usefulness of all dimensions of the evaluation process. In each chapter descriptions and considerations have focused your attention on a variety of roles which the teacher is expected to assume. Removed from the classroom setting you were urged to isolate specific behaviors and to analyze both the affective and cognitive effects of these on teaching and learning. This final exercise urges the results of the Interaction Activities to extend beyond this beginning period and to influence teacher practices. Success depends on your relating the process employed in these activities with subsequent professional situations. Beginning teachers are encouraged to view themselves as unique contributors to evolving educational systems, rather than patterning their practices on what already exists. Without assistance and support from supervisors, beginning teachers are unlikely to perceive professional objectives generalizable beyond the one or more schools assigned them during this beginning-teacher phase.

Directions and Procedures

[Leader establishes the appropriate setting for this activity and distributes a 3 x 5 index card to each participant.]

Leader: You have come to the culminating exercises in this experience. Stating goals, planning strategies, examining evidence are some of the performance areas you have demonstrated. In what ways will you continue gaining additional teaching competencies? The following Interaction Activity invites you to reflect on your teaching abilities and personal characteristics.

Take the card and mark it creating above and below-the-line areas. You determine where the line should be located. Above the line, list the specific abilities and strengths you realize you have--personal and professional--which contribute to your effectiveness as a teacher. Below the line list specific areas in which you realize you need improvement--personal and professional areas you perceive as weak. Although you have expended effort in acquiring certain behaviors, you recognize the need for additional practice. The card is for your viewing only. Allow time for thoughtful and spontaneous writing rejecting no words or phrases.

[After participants have completed the card, invite all to contribute to the large-group discussion.]

Discussion Questions

Leader: Looking at your card, at the position of your line, and the labeling in each area of this card, I am going to ask you to talk about the activity. Since you have been in similar situations, I am asking you to share as a large group rather than to first talk with one person. First, how would you describe the kind of line you made? Is it straight? Jagged? Slanted? Was it drawn lightly? Strong and dark? Where is the line now as compared with your placing it some weeks ago?

Next, I would like you to re-examine the labeling above and below the line. In what ways are they alike? Different? To what extent are you comfortable identifying your abilities? Weaknesses? In what ways has self assessment changed your teaching performance?

SKILL ACTIVITY: **Assessing Teaching Performance**

Objectives
To demonstrate ability to evaluate self performance as teacher.
To assess relationship of instruction to learner performance.

Self evelution is essential to progress and achievement of teaching competencies. Presenting specific skills for practice has offered you the opportunity to become a competent teacher. Supervising and other teachers have encouraged and reinforced your effort. Suggestions have been made and followed by shared evaluative reporting. Nevertheless, for continuous growth in becoming an effective teacher, self evaluation is necessary.

Throughout this teaching experience the activities emphasized reflection and examination of your teaching behaviors. Shared discussion evoked diversity of attitude, opinion and ideas regarding educational theory and practice. In this culminating assignment you logged comments on specific components of your instructional performance. The exercise assisted you in developing keen self-evaluative skill, thus increasing your potential for becoming an effective teacher.

The following questions may be used in group discussion or in private conference with the supervisor:

1. To what extent did you consider the varied learner capabilities in preparation for this lesson? How are you providing for the individual learner?
2. Do the materials and procedures match your objectives for the lesson taught? What is the learning value of this lesson?
3. What was your rationale for selecting the assessment device used for this lesson? Could other devices be used as well? How will you use the assessment results?
4. What are your strengths in your teaching performance? You may want to focus on one lesson then generalize to other classes taught.
5. What are your weaknesses? You may find it easier to express the weaknesses, nevertheless the improvement and attainment of competencies is the emphasis.
6. What makes the difference between you at this point, and an interested adult who could follow an instruction manual in the classroom? What makes you "teacher?" What knowledge and skills are essential to the role of teacher?

Preparation for Teaching Positions

Inquiry about Positions
You are now ready to make inquiry about possible teaching positions within the school system of your choice. Most school systems require an application form to be completed. These forms may be requested by mail or phone from the Personnel Director. Your letter of inquiry and/or application form should be typewritten or printed neatly and free from grammatical errors (*check spelling and punctuation).

Interviewing for Positions
Contact with the prospective employer will most likely culminate in an interview session. A successful interview is contingent upon the preparation and anticipation of questions which the interviewer will ask. The following questions are provided to use either as a role playing activity or for your preparation.

1. What specific talents do you bring to the teaching profession that will benefit students?

_____

_____

_____

2. To what extent do you believe a teacher's self concept influences students?

_____

_____

_____

3. What are your feelings and policies concerning discipline and classroom management?

_____

_____

_____

4. How do you think students learn?

_____

_____

_____

5. What type of community and school are you looking for in seeking a position?

_____

_____

_____

6. How prepared are you to work with varied learner abilities?

_____

_____

_____

7. To what extent do you value observations by supervisors and principals?

_____

_____

_____

8. How many students can you manage effectively in a class?

_____

_____

_____

9. What types of individualized materials have you made and/or used?

_____

_____

_____

10. Are you interested in working with students in an extra/co-curricular activity?

_____

_____

_____

In addition to preparing for the response to questions by the interviewer you might generate a list to ask the interviewer such as:

1. What types of in-service and supervisory programs does the school system provide?

2. Is there a general school system policy on discipline, grading, homework?

3. What is the beginning teacher's salary? Are salary increments based on merit pay or career ladder concepts?

4. What is the school system policy for teacher evaluation?

Keep in mind that an interview is significant to the hiring of new personnel. It is important that you arrive promptly for your appointment, dress professionally and speak to the interviewer with clear and distinct language.

*You make take any of the following for possible examination by the interviewer: transcript, resume, application form, sample lesson plans, learner packet/center or unit materials and VCR tape recording of lesson presentation. The placement office on the college or university campus usually provides sample copies of inquiry letters and resume's. You may want to attend training sessions preparing candidates for interviews.

Obtaining Certification

Certification is required of public school teachers in the fifty states and the District of Columbia. Due to recent and extensive changes in teacher certification you are advised to contact the department of education in the state you are seeking employment. The teacher certification official in the school of education can provide a listing of certification requirements and addresses of the teacher certification officer of each state. Prior to completing your preparation program you could obtain the listing of certification requirements and examine each one. If standardized tests are included, note the complete name of the test, dates and locations of test sights. Whether it be initial certification or one for a specialized area you can locate the state's procedure for issuing a license to teach.

Continuing Professional Development

Keeping abreast of current issues and trends in a particular teaching level and discipline can be accomplished in many ways. In addition to inservice provided you on theories and new instructional strategies by the school system employing you, there are organizations and groups at the local, state, regional and national levels promoting teacher growth. These professional organizations offer its members a variety of resources through journals and other publications and through regular scheduled meetings. Although membership applications can be obtained for any desired level, the titles and addresses of the national offices of selected professional organizations are given below:

American Federation of Teachers
    11 DuPont Circle, N.W., Washington, D.C. 20036

American Association of Elementary-Kindergarten and Nursery Education
    1201 Sixteenth Street, N.W., Washington, D.C. 20036

American Historical Association
    400 A Street, S.E., Washington, D.C. 20003

Council for Education of the Deaf
    Ralph Hoag, Post Office Box 5545, Tucson, Arizona 85703

Council for Exceptional Children
    1920 Association Drive, Reston, Virginia 22091

International Reading Association
  800 Bardsdale Road, Newark, Delaware 19711

Music Educators National Conference
  1902 Association Drive, Reston, Virginia 22091

National Art Education Association
  1916 Association Drive, Reston, Virginia 22091

National Business Education Association
  1906 Association Drive, Reston, Virginia 22091

National Council of Teachers of English
  508 South Sixth Street, Champaign, Illinois 61820

National Council of Teachers of Mathematics
  1906 Association Drive, Reston, Virginaia 22091

National Council for the Social Studies
  2030 M Street, N.W., Washington, D.C. 20036

National Education Association
  1201 16th Street N.W., Washington, D.C. 20036

National Science Teachers Association
  1742 Connecticut Avenue, N.W., Washington, D.C. 20009

Continuing Effective Teaching

   Through the activities within each chapter you have been encouraged to practice specific communication and instructional skills basic to becoming an effective teacher. In addition, you have discovered the influence of district and school administration on the school environment, organization and instructional process. Equipped with the teaching knowledge, skill and an understanding of the variety of influences which impact the instructional process you are prepared to make your contribution to the education profession.

APPENDIX A

One-Way Communication

Directions The person who directs the activity should read all instructions before beginning. The object of the activity is to give clear, verbal descriptions allowing participants to hear all that is spoken. Take whatever time is needed to do this. The director's voice is the only source of the message.

First, situate yourself in the same room as the other participants and behind a screen or some furniture which prevents you and the other participants from seeing each other.

Second, take a few minutes to decide how you will describe this diagram to the group. They will draw what you tell them.

Third, begin the directions, using the explanations which would best help them draw the design shown below. Neither you nor they may ask each other questions.

The <u>leader</u> collects the diagrams and assigns scores--one point for each correctly positioned figure.

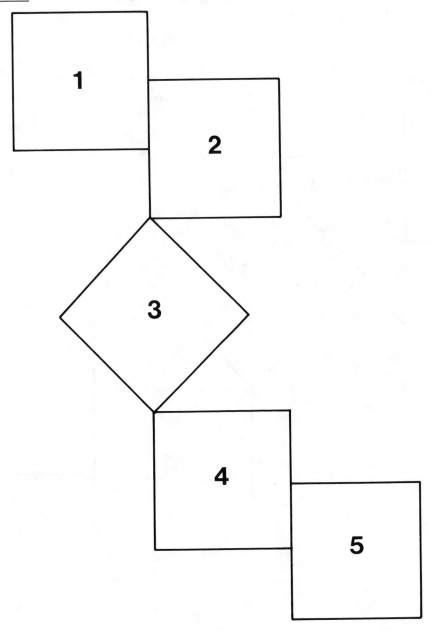

Two-Way Communication

Directions For this activity the director and participants are visible to each other. The object is that both the director and recipients verbally interact while accomplishing the assigned task.

First, situate yourself in front of the participants.

Second, hold this diagram so that it is not visible to participants from beneath or on either side.

Third, begin the directions, using the explanation which would best help the participants to draw the design shown below. They may ask you for verbal information and you may answer their questions. No gestures or visual representations may be given.

After participants and director are satisfied with the instructions, the leader collects the diagrams and assigns scores--one point for each correctly positioned figure. Scores for the One and Two-Way Communication can be compared.

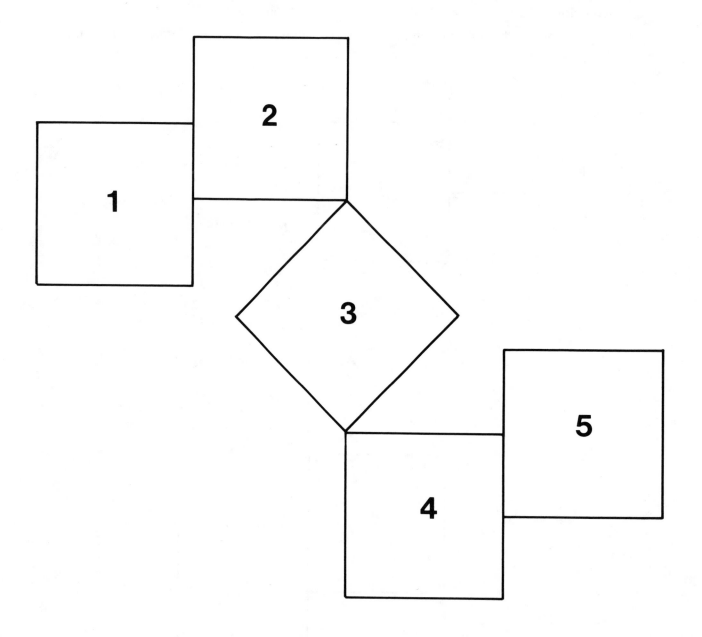

APPENDIX B

Diagrams for the Interaction Activity: Cooperating and Coping

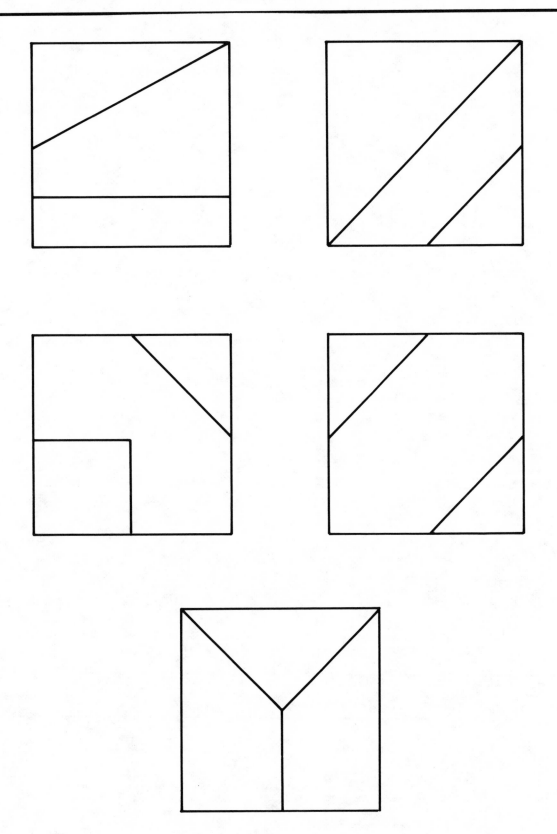

Index

About the Authors

Serra Goethals is Professor of Education and currently Chairperson of the Education Department at Bellarmine College. She received her Ph.D. in Curriculum and Instruction from George Peabody College for Teachers of Vanderbilt University. Her teaching experience spans elementary, junior high and college levels and she has been principal of an elementary school. Advisor, teacher, supervisor and consultant, she is involved in the public and parochial school systems.

Dr. Goethals frequently conducts workshops for teachers, principals and parents, develops teacher education programs, authors grants to support the preparation of special educators and serves on numerous local and state boards and committees representing various educational constituencies.

Rose A. Howard received her Ph.D. in Curriculum and Instruction and Ed.S. in Counselor Education from George Peabody College for Teachers of Vanderbilt University. Currently Director of Secondary Education at Bellarmine College, Dr. Howard has been a teacher at the elementary, junior and senior high school levels and has also been a school principal.

Professor of Education, Dr. Howard advises, teaches, supervises and consults with middle and high school teachers. She has authored articles in Clearing House and Phi Delta Kappan, co-authored handbooks, presented workshops for teachers and administrators on the national, state and local levels and is a frequent consultant to high school administrators.